Kentucky Theatre Yearbook 2016

Bill McCann, Jr., Editor

JW Books
Cynthiana, KY

© 2016 by JW Books, Cynthiana, Kentucky   All Rights Reserved

Cover Photo: Photograph by Mikki Schaffner Photography http://mikkischaffner.com. Copyright © 2016 by Philip Paradis. (Left to right) Carter Bratton and Robert Macke in Soldier's Christmas by Phil Paradis, at Corbett Theater, Northern Kentucky University, Highland Heights, KY 41099 December 12, 2014.

Amateurs and professionals are hereby notified that the version of *Sunny Side* © 2015 by Philip Paradis appearing in this journal is a literary version only. Appearance in this book does not give readers the right to perform the play without the express consent of the author and upon payment of appropriate royalties. (See page 144 for information about performance rights to this play.)

Amateurs and professionals are hereby notified that the version of *Dividing Adam's Ashes* © 2015 by A.K. Forbes appearing in this journal is a literary version only. Appearance in this book does not give readers the right to perform the play without the express consent of the author and upon payment of appropriate royalties. (See page 144 for information about performance rights to this play.)

Warning: All Rights Reserved. No part of the Kentucky Theatre Yearbook, 2016 may be reproduced, stored in a retrieval system, or transmitted in any form or by any means, whether electronic, mechanical, photocopying, recording, or otherwise, without the express prior written permission of the publisher. The unauthorized reproduction or distribution of this copyrighted work, in whole or in part, is illegal and forbidden. Inquiries regarding reproduction or distribution should be addressed to the publishers: JW Books, Rights Enquiry, PO Box 143, Cynthiana, KY 41031.

Journalists, critics, and teachers may use short excerpts in critical essays and for classroom purposes only, under "Fair Use" provisions of the copyright law.

Submit articles and reviews to ky.playwright@yahoo.com with title of article or review in the subject line.

Submit queries with clippings to Bill McCann, Jr, Editor KTY, JW Books, PO 143 Cynthiana, KY 41031

**Dedicated to
Marsha Norman**

Contents

Introduction by Bill McCann, Jr. 6

Who is a Kentucky Playwright? by Bill McCann, Jr. 9

The Dramatists Guild: Advocate and Resource for Playwrights by Nancy Gall-Clayton 11

Looking to the Past to Find Our Future by Michael W. Hatton 15

The Best Training for a Playwright by Steve Cleberg .. 25

Inside a Director's Head by Steve Cleberg. 27

Dividing Adam's Ashes: A Short Play by A.K. Forbes .. 30

Sunny Side: A Ten-Minute Comedy for Two Actors by Philip Paradis 42

The Kentucky New Plays Census by Bill McCann, Jr. 50

Part One: Plays Given Readings or Performances 51

    Productions in Kentucky by Kentucky Playwrights 51

    Kentucky Playwrights with Productions Outside Kentucky 72

    Kentucky Playwrights with Readings in Kentucky 79

    Kentucky Playwrights with Readings Outside Kentucky 83

    Awards 87

    Part Two: Theatres 90

        Kentucky Theatres that Produced New Plays...90

        New Plays Produced at Non-Traditional
        Theatres/Venues in Kentucky 105

        New Plays by Kentucky Playwrights Performed
        at Theatres/Venues Outside Kentucky.............107

        New Plays by Kentucky Playwrights Performed
        at Non-Traditional Theatres/Venues Outside
        Kentucky 118

Playwright Support and Training 119

Kentucky Contests, Festivals, and Opportunities 122

Kentucky Venues for Self-Producing Playwrights 129

Contributors 132

Appendix: Historical Data 134

The Next Issue 139

Help Wanted 142

Notices 144

Submissions 144

About the Editor 146

Introduction
by Bill McCann, Jr.

This book has been two years in coming, a work of love and dedication, not only by myself and those who worked directly on compiling and writing the information it contains, but most especially the playwrights who authored the plays at the heart of this book. Without playwrights there would be no theatre and nowhere is that clearer than on the pages devoted to the Kentucky New Plays Census: 2014 and 2015.

The Census documents what those of us involved in Kentucky theatre have long known: Kentucky's theatre scene is vital and alive because of talented playwrights and many theatres that produced the work of those playwrights. As of today there are about 131 professional, semi-professional, summer stock and community theatres located in 55 of Kentucky's 120 counties. Surprisingly, there are about an equal number of playwrights in and from this state whose work can be found on stages here and elsewhere around the world. And the more than 30 Kentucky theatres that produce new works are to be commended for giving opportunities to our playwrights.

Some Kentucky playwrights are world famous and acclaimed—Pulitzer Prize winning playwrights John Patrick, Marsha Norman and Suzan-Lori Parks come to mind, as do Sallie Bingham, George C. Wolfe, Naomi Wallace, and Maurine Dallas Watkins. But most toil at learning their craft, seeking productions of works that embody their heart and soul with fame and fortune never coming for them outside the bosom of the community that they call home.

It is hoped that this book and its future editions change theatre and change Kentucky. By bringing awareness to the state's playwrights it is hoped that more of them will have their plays produced. By publishing plays by two playwrights from Northern Kentucky—A.K. Forbes and Phil Paradis—it is hoped that students of playwriting will become acquainted with, perhaps inspired by, the work of fellow playwrights even as they attempt to discover for themselves what works, and what doesn't in the plays they read. Further, it is hoped that these plays will join those published elsewhere in inspiring our playwrights to work on their craft, to aspire not merely to be writers of plays but playwrights. Over time, it can be hoped that Kentucky playwrights like Doug Schutte, Nancy Gall-Clayton, Elizabeth Orendorff, Phil Paradis, Larry Muhammad, and readers of this book will impact the world of theatre far beyond the bounds of Kentucky, even as Kentucky's past Pulitzer and Tony winning playwrights already have.

Try as I might, spending two years doing so, this book is still incomplete. I am sure that not all plays given readings and productions in Kentucky have been included in the listings. So there is reason to believe that with this as a starting point, future issues will get better. Over time a greater variety of articles about theatre in Kentucky will appear within these pages. For instance, next year's issue will feature Kentucky Chautauqua, sponsored by the Kentucky Humanities Council, whose playwright-actors bring to life characters from our common history. Beyond covering theatre generally, we will always strive to document all of the plays given readings and productions as a way to help and inspire our state's playwrights—the heart of any theatre community. Finally, the information in the Appendix—historical data—will be continually expanded and updated to help scholars study and write about Kentucky theatre.

The ambitions of this book are beyond the reality of the current volume. But over time the book will improve and expand. It will provide advertising for theatres, for university and college theatre programs to reach potential students, and it will be a forum for Kentucky playwrights to promote themselves and their work. It will seek to become the authoritative resource about what has happened and what is going to happen across Kentucky, in theatres and venues that produce theatrical productions. Give us your feedback. Submit reviews of new works you see, scripts of plays you'd like to see published. Let us know about theatrical trends and interests in your part of Kentucky or the world of theatre more broadly conceived.

One last comment. This book has involved the help and support of many people, including all of the authors whose articles and plays are contained here; the beta readers Nancy Gall-Clayton, Elizabeth Shear Orendorff, Phil Paradis, and Doug Schutte; and folks who have provided information about their productions or readings as well as information about the work of others, including Trish Ayers, Sarah Diamond Burroway, Michael Bigelow Dixon, Liz Fentress, Herman Farrell, Robby Henson, Jim Inman, Kristi Johnson, Kim Miller, Brian Walker, and I am sure far more people than that. I apologize to those I have inadvertently left unmentioned. And most importantly of all, I thank Jeanine Grant Lister, whose wonderfully supportive attitude is only exceed by the exactitude of her copy editing abilities. Even with all of this help there will inevitably be mistakes and omissions; for those I accept all blame.

Who is a Kentucky Playwright?
by Bill McCann, Jr.

As is so often the case, the obvious may not be obvious. In preparing the list of plays written by Kentucky playwrights, I was faced with defining "Kentucky playwright," and to some degree I failed. Ultimately each person defines how they see themselves; each playwright decides whether he or she is a Kentucky playwright. On Derby Day I suspect that everyone who absorbs the melancholy longing in the words to "My Old Kentucky Home" is a Kentuckian.

Still, for purposes of this essay and the listings that follow, a Kentucky playwright is an individual who tells Kentucky's stories using dialogue with the intention that the work be to be performed.

Ah, were it that simple.

It seems obvious that a playwright who *lives* in a state is a playwright of that state. Those living in Lexington, Louisville, Dry Ridge, Corinth, Paducah, or Pikeville, or elsewhere in the state are Kentucky playwrights. But who else qualifies to submit plays to contests or theatres that accept scripts only from Kentucky playwrights?

Someone who has never lived in Kentucky may be a Kentucky playwright if he or she has been highly influenced by experiences that in turn influence their plays. A graduate of any of the state's public or private colleges or universities is a Kentucky playwright. Someone who was born, grew up, and graduated from one of the state's high schools qualifies; the same is true of someone who was born here.

Yet there are also instances of people qualifying as Kentucky playwrights because, though they were not born here, their plays have been influenced by a Kentucky heritage or an interest in telling Kentucky stories. Arlene Hutton writes many plays which are Kentucky plays: *The Nibroc Trilogy* and *As it is in Heaven* are set in Kentucky and reflect the influence of having spent a great deal of her childhood on her grandparents' farm near Corbin. On the other hand, Toronto-born playwright Michael Ross Albert might well be considered a Kentucky playwright because his trilogy *The Big Sandy River Plays* is set in Eastern Kentucky; these commissioned plays premiered at Jenny Wiley Theatre between 2012 and 2015 and well reflect the state in which they are set.

And then there is the question of plays written about Kentucky, set in Kentucky—such as Robert Schenkkan's *The Kentucky Cycle*—but which are arguably based on negative stereotypes of Kentuckians. Is Robert Schenkkan—one of our nation's best known and well thought of playwrights—a Kentucky playwright? *The Kentucky Cycle* won a Pulitzer Prize. Is Robert Schenkkan a Kentucky playwright, or does the fact that his play is found lacking by many Kentuckians a reason to think otherwise?

What do you think? Let the cussin' an' feudin' begin!

The Dramatists Guild: Advocate and Resource for Playwrights
by Nancy Gall-Clayton

Almost 7,200 playwrights, librettists, lyricists, and composers—including 50 who live in Kentucky—belong to the Dramatists Guild. The Guild was founded in 1912 to "protect and promote the interests of the men and women who write for the stage." No other organization has this mission.

New National Focus

For many years, the Guild focused on the needs and concerns of New York-based playwrights. However, a major shift has occurred, and the DG now works very intentionally to make itself relevant and beneficial to members no matter where they live.

Twenty-nine regional representatives ("reps") have been appointed to organize one gathering in their areas each year to bring playwrights together for theatre, workshops, and other events. Reps also do research in their geographic areas, most recently for "The Count," a study documenting the gender and race of playwrights produced at major theatres in this country over a three-year period. In addition, reps write three reports a year about activities in their regions for *The Dramatist*, the Guild's bimonthly magazine. The organization has also begun to host national conferences. To draw participants from all regions, the first three biennial conferences were held in Chicago and on each coast.

Kentucky Focus

Kentucky has its own representative, thanks to Herman Daniel Farrell III, who lobbied the national office for one and was appointed as our first rep. I followed him, beginning my three-year term in spring of 2014. Also serving Kentucky is a Youth Ambassador. Lexington-based Elizabeth "Ellie" Kilcoyne was the first person in that role. In 2016, Jackson Wolford of Louisville was appointed as Kentucky's Youth Ambassador. Youth Ambassadors work with their reps on various activities and provide a different perspective on how to serve the needs of writers in their areas.

What the Dramatists Guild Does

The Guild and its Legal Defense Fund are fierce advocates for playwrights, particularly around copyright infringement and censorship. Enter John Cariana whose four-page article in the July/August 2015 issue of *The Dramatist* describes how officials at Maiden High School in Maiden, North Carolina, canceled his play *Almost, Maine* for "sexually explicit overtones." When these officials were unmoved by an outpouring of community support for a school production, the play was produced privately after a highly successful Kickstarter campaign.

North Carolina's Guild rep, Kim Stinson, will speak about the Guild's involvement in the cancelation and subsequent production of *Almost, Maine* at the 2016 Southeastern Theatre Conference convention. Kim's remarks will be part of a presentation about the Guild's work, with DG representatives from Baltimore and Colorado, and myself as her co-panelists.

Guild Publications

In addition to articles like the one concerning censorship in North Carolina, *The Dramatist* also includes essays by and interviews with writers and composers like A.R. Gurney, Tina Howe, Sarah Ruhl, Arthur Miller, Marsha Norman, Stephen Schwartz, and Doug Wright.

Recent themed issues have been on Musical Theatre, Writers and Directors, and Devised Theatre. One of my favorite features in *The Dramatist* is a column by Gary Garrison, Executive Director of Creative Affairs, who just happens to be the most creative thinker I know. (If you write short plays, do read Gary's book *Perfect 10: Writing and Producing the 10-Minute Play*.)

In addition to *The Dramatist*, the Guild has an online eNewsletter with up-to-the-minute news, submission opportunities, and reports from members about readings, productions, and awards. And of course, there's the Guild's concise Bill of Rights outlining what a playwright should expect when a play or musical is chosen for production.

Other Perks of Membership

The Guild will review—at no charge—a member's unsigned contract to see if it meets industry standards. A member from Kentucky was impressed by the speedy and professional response provided when he contacted them in 2015 requesting this service. Further, model contracts are available without charge from the Business Office.

Members have access to an online directory of submission opportunities and may post their profiles on the Guild website. There's virtual access to DG Huddles— informal video conversations—about topics like indie funding, measuring success, time management, and networking. Also available for online listening are dozens of podcasts featuring conversations with prominent writers for the stage.

Yet another member perk is the Friday Night Footlights Program, which allows Guild members free use of a room at its offices in Manhattan for readings of new work. The Kentucky Women Playwrights Seminar in Berea took advantage of this opportunity to present their play *Shh!* in 2014.

Kentucky Networking Opportunities

Herman Farrell set up a Facebook page for us titled "Dramatists Guild—Kentucky Region" where members can share theatre news, and also become aware of one another.

I've organized two Guild events in Kentucky, one in Berea and one in Highland Heights. Berea College's Chair of Theatre, DG member Shan Ayers, arranged for free and discounted tickets to see Naomi Wallace's play *The Trestle at Pope Lick Creek* at the college, and we gathered for brunch and conversation the next morning.

At a luncheon at Northern Kentucky University, Michael W. Hatton, Head of Theatre and Dance at NKU's School of the Arts, spoke about his program, the only one in Kentucky offering a Bachelor of Fine Arts in Playwriting.

When this book went to print, a regional event was planned for February 28, 2016. Members and those considering joining the Guild were invited to a celebratory reception at Louisville's Bunbury Theatre to honor Walter May and to see his play *Gone Astray*, which besides being written by a Kentucky Guild member, features Liz Fentress, another Kentucky Guild member, in the cast.

How to Join

If you are a playwright, composer, lyricist, or librettist, consider becoming part of our community and enjoying the benefits of membership in the Dramatists Guild. Visit http://www.dramatistsguild.com for more information. Feel free to email me if you have questions at ngallclayton@dramatistsguild.com.

Looking to the Past to Find Our Future
by Michael W. Hatton

Editor's Note: The following is a speech given to Kentucky members of the Dramatists Guild meeting at Northern Kentucky University, Summer 2015.

Good morning. On behalf of the faculty and staff of Northern Kentucky University's Theatre and Dance Program, it is my pleasure to welcome you to our campus. We are so very honored to host you and I am pleased to share with you the exciting and meaningful work that is occurring at NKU.

In preparing to speak with you today, I explored the history of the Dramatists Guild and the purpose for its creation. To quote from the Guild's website, "The Guild believes that a vibrant, vital and provocative theater is an essential element of the ongoing cultural debate which informs the citizens of a free society. The Guild believes that if such a theater is to survive, the unique, idiosyncratic voices of both men and women who write for it must be cultivated and protected."

Students, leaders, and members alike often forget to occasionally revisit the core ideas and values of their organization or institution. We sometimes take for granted the privileges that have become second nature or feel overly confident in our ability to interpret the dreams and goals of our founding members. I'm reminded of a scene from the television series *The West Wing* in which the embattled President Josiah Bartlett stands at the foot of the Lincoln Memorial gazing up at the statue's marble face.

Having been urged to go and "listen to Lincoln" by a former President, the character of Bartlett takes a moment to reflect upon the values, traditions, and future of both his presidency and the nation.

Like the character of President Bartlett, the Theatre and Dance Program at NKU asks our students to reflect upon the tradition of theatre, to explore the multiple facets that exist with the art form, and to begin imagining a future in which they become leaders and push to shape the scope and scale of theatre. This three-part journey is certainly not easy but it begins by sharing the belief of the Dramatists Guild that the voices of our students should be cultivated and protected.

As a liberal arts institution, our theatre majors have the opportunity to connect disparate ideas, practice trans-disciplinarity, and prepare themselves to be active and responsible citizens of the world. While these goals sound lofty, they are rooted in the very sincere belief that success in life comes from the skills we learn, the relationships that we form, and the appreciation of diversity we cultivate. I share with parents and students alike that art cannot be created in a bubble and that the liberal arts experience can have a tremendous impact upon the work they do while in college and especially within their lives and careers post college. For us as a program though, the imperative goes further, and it must go further still. For our students to create lasting, sustaining, and challenging theatre, they must endeavor to explore the world and to better themselves in the process by becoming good writers, by learning to think critically, and never losing sight of the humanity which stands at the core of our art. It is these elements which allow for the meaningful participation in that ongoing cultural debate and the crafting of a free society.

    We accomplish these goals in a variety of ways but there are four of which I am most proud. First, we embrace the study of theatre across cultures and time periods in our curriculum to better understand the humanity from which our art springs forth. From the Aristotelian treatise on the dramatic structure to the Neoclassical Ideals, students learn from where theatre has come and with this new-found appreciation they can begin the work of borrowing, adapting, and bending the rules. Through our study abroad programs students are immersed in the landscapes of canonical plays and the stories come alive like never before. Whether it be the Caribbean, Greece, or the United Kingdom, our students don't just observe, they integrate these experiences into their art.

    In my Dramatic Theory and Criticism course, one of our program's BFA playwriting students, Syreeta Briggs, expressed the dilemma of creating a diverse theatre in this way:

> If theatre is to be a mirror, merely reflecting the society in which it is born into, why not have the protagonist be a person of color? Or someone of the LGBTQ community? As an artist, a playwright, and a lover of theatre I find it my duty and the duty of every budding theatre artist around me to change his or her vocabulary when speaking of diversity in regards to the theatre. Instead of declaring that we, today's budding theatre artists/activists, are out 'to diversify' theatre, let us begin saying that we are simply out to normalize it. In reference to television writer

Shonda Rhimes, we must finally make theatre 'look the way the world looks' and 'diversify' suggests including characters who are women, or of color, or homosexual, or even a combination of the three.... And from this moment forward it must be made clear that our quest is simply to have our theatre look the way our world looks.

As a program in the new NKU School of the Arts we are working to address the issues raised by Miss Briggs by aligning one of our program's core practices with one of our core philosophies. It is vital that students be exposed to the full breadth and depth of dramatic literature. We celebrate a revisionist historiography which means that the plays we study in class and produce on stage should not be limited to playwrights most commonly identified as white, male, and heterosexual.

During the four year tenure of students in our program, we endeavor to produce plays and musicals from each major time period and from each major style through a rotating formulaic schedule. While the effort has been successful, there is still much work to be done. The low enrollment of minority students within our program and university has often hindered the ability to present plays and musicals which feature non-White characters and storylines. We then suffer from the cyclical issue of students not seeing themselves represented on stage as they are in real life. When you don't see yourself represented you migrate towards communities and organizations where you do see yourself. More can be done and more will be done to ensure that all students see representation of themselves on our stages and in the dramatic literature we study.

A third way in which our program seeks to have students connect disparate ideas and practice trans-disciplinarity comes in the form of our Konstantinow Studio Series and First Year Show. We believe that freshmen should be given every opportunity to explore dramatic literature and to begin analyzing and performing it as early as possible. While in the safe environment of the rehearsal studio, we push students to triumph magnificently or to flop hard…and then get up off the ground and try again. In their first semester as freshmen, we produce the aptly titled First Year Show, a mainstage production in which they have tackled the works of Aristophanes, Sophocles, Miller, Carroll, and Wedekind. Not only does this production bond the freshman class and help them to become grounded in their work, but they begin to see that what they thought they knew about theatre is only the tip of the iceberg.

The Konstaninow Studio Series, on the other hand, is the laboratory of our upper-level students where the practice of trans-disciplinarity and critical thinking truly take hold. Each year, the Studio Series produces 4 to 10 student productions in which all facets of the production, from directing to design, is handled by the students. It is in this series that students can go further with content than we might normally be able to do in our mainstage season. The ramifications of season selection and planning are something which students must practice as part of the practical application of theatre management skills and real-world scenarios. But what truly makes the studio series shine is the frequent presentation of new works.

It is important for the students in our BFA playwriting program to have their new plays developed and produced in our experimental laboratory. The studio series gives the playwrights an opportunity to not only be a part of the rehearsal process but to experience their play in a fleshed-out and fully-produced way. As a director, I have had the privilege of working with several of our playwrights as they fine-tune and hone their work. The learning experience does not stop with the playwright either. Student directors, student designers, and yes, even student dramaturgs collaborate together and experiment in creating the new works which will contribute to our ongoing cultural debate and shape the future of theatre.

If there is one way, however, that our program significantly aligns itself with the Dramatists Guild's mission to promote vibrant, vital, and provocative theatre, it is through the production of our biennial YES Festival of New Plays. Over the past 34 years, NKU Theatre and Dance has produced over fifty new works and received submissions from playwrights in Cincinnati all the way to Siberia. Planning for the YES festival begins about 18 months prior to the festival with prospective plays arriving 11 months in advance of the opening night. Three plays or musicals are selected to receive a fully-staged world premiere and the plays cannot have had any professional staging in order to be considered. Once the three finalists have been selected the playwrights are in residence at NKU in the final days of the rehearsal process. The playwrights are able to see their works fully realized and given the opportunity to make adjustments to the text as desired. Working on a new text is both exciting and daunting for our students. The opportunity to create a character and bring them to life for the very first time is an experience that has a profound effect upon the developing artistic process of the actors. Similarly, they approach the roles with great respect as they know the playwrights are still crafting their plays. So few actors, directors, and designers get to work on a new play in this type of intimate environment. It is truly inspiring and humbling to support the work of playwrights and to be so closely involved with the development of dramatic literature.

The importance of the work that our program does in conjunction with the YES Festival and the support of playwrights was made ever clearer with this year's presentation of the Tony Awards. To the dismay of many theatre artists, CBS chose to present major awards in playwriting during commercial breaks, thus negating their importance to viewers. Current Dramatists Guild President, Doug Wright, put it best when he wrote, "Every year, the Academy Awards faithfully includes screenwriters in not one but two categories. And it's not just the Oscars; the Grammys, Emmys and Golden Globes all award the writers in their respective industries on the air. Ironically it's the theater that most esteems writers; we are generally recognized as the principal artistic force behind new work, and we even retain ownership and control over the material we create. Yet on the very awards show intended to celebrate our craft, we are effectively negated."

Mr. Wright is referring to a cultural climate in the United States which is becoming increasingly hostile to intellectual pursuits. In this cultural climate, it then becomes even more important to support the work of our playwrights. The idea that higher education, the social sciences, and God forbid, the arts can contribute to a person's development and personal success has slowly, but markedly, been supplanted with the idea that success equals having a marketable set of skills which lead to a high-paying job. The skills required for success in the arts, collaboration, creativity, discipline, critical thinking, are eschewed as being elitist and not worthy of attention.

In an article for *The Huffington Post*, West Chester University Professor of Anthropology Paul Stoller takes anti-intellectuals to task by saying:

> In the past, 'can do' pragmatism was the fuel of American prosperity. But that pragmatism was reinforced with an abiding respect for knowledge and critical thinking. In the past we knew that it was hard to do anything in a place devoid of new ideas, a place where dreamers are discouraged from dreaming. That's why in the present it's important to combat the anti-intellectualism of the public sphere and support enlightened higher education, a space where mentors, to borrow from one of my readers, don't teach students what to think but show them how to think—a skill that prepares them for a productive life in the world, a skill that moves all of us forward.

It is with this desire to move forward and to help students become critical thinkers and artists that NKU made an exciting change this past July with the creation of a new School of the Arts. This past year all three fine arts programs conducted internal reviews to determine whether or not we are preparing artists capable of contributing to our society and disciplines. The NKU Theatre and Dance Program serves 303 theatre majors and 57 theatre minors, making us one of the largest programs on campus. We offer two bachelor's degrees, one in theatre and the other in theatre in world cultures, while also offering seven BFA degrees in theatre, with tracks in acting, musical theatre, dance, design or technology, rock and roll/concert technology, stage management, and perhaps most important of all, playwriting.

Are our graduates finding success post-graduation? Yes. Now, more than ever before, our graduates are finding success on Broadway, on regional tours, on cruise ships, in film and television, in graduate school, as teachers, as husbands, wives, business leaders, community leaders, and supporters of the arts. Can we find new ways to equip them to handle the unique demands that they will encounter in the next fifty years? Yes. We believe that merging the programs of theatre and dance, music, and visual arts into a new School of the Arts is the best way to service future generations of students and ensure continued success. Breaking down the traditional barriers which separate our disciplines will allow students to tap into new avenues of artistry, develop collaborations which were previously impossible, and take our creativity to the next level. Our plans include the development of a new interdisciplinary degree which will allow students to develop art using multiple media while preparing them for the demands of ever changing industries. The hope is that the new School of the Arts will continue to grow over time and perhaps become home to new programs such as Architecture, Culinary Arts, and Arts Therapy. The possibilities are endless.

While the future is wide open and it's a very exciting time to be a part of the School of the Arts, the need to keep our students at the heart of everything we do becomes more important than ever. Student success is key and augmenting the ability of students to create art with fewer boundaries is our goal. With society continually fluctuating and a constant state of change becoming the new normal, it is easy to forget why we became storytellers. We forget why we need to tell stories and to share in the communal experience of theatre. As teachers, playwrights, students, and artists, we mustn't lose sight of these moments. While each of us often reflects upon our artistry and the work we do in theatre, I encourage you to remember the primal nature and simple pleasures our work can provide. I leave you with this quote from theatre designer Robert Edmund Jones:

> Many thousands of years have passed since that first moment of inspiration when the theatre sprang into being. But we still like to get together, we still dread to be alone, we are still a little awed by silence, we still like to make believe, and when an artist like Duse or Chaliapin or Pauline Lord speaks aloud in our midst a thing that is in the minds of all of us and fuses our various moods into one common mood, we are still lost in wonder before this magical art of the theatre. It is really a kind of magic, this art. We call it glamour or poetry or romance, but that doesn't explain it. In some mysterious way these old, simple, ancestral moods still survive in us, and an actor can make them live again for a while. We become children once more. We believe.

The Best Training for a Playwright
by Steve Cleberg

Most choose to be writers because they are burning to tell their stories. The literary artist chronicles their passions on the page in hopes that they will inspire the kindred souls who read their work. After their work is completed, they seek credibility by entering writing contests and competitions. The ultimate goal for the literary artist is publication leading to widespread recognition.

Literary art has the potential for a very wide audience culled over a long period of time. On the other hand, the performing arts are ephemeral in nature. That is to say that they exist only as they are created. True, the script is an artifact that remains after the play is complete but it's a mere fragment of the complete theatre artwork.

Playwriting isn't a literary art; it's one of the design processes for a performing art. Playwrights are not literary artists who are set apart from the process of theatre. Shakespeare and Moliere began their careers as actors, learning the basic craft of theatre, before they began writing for the stage. Henrik Ibsen wrote many unsuccessful plays as a young man. Only after he was involved in staging over a hundred plays at a Swedish theatre did he go on to write some of the greatest dramas ever written.

Even the word "playwright" connotes a builder rather than an author. Much in the same way that a shipwright engages in the craft of building and launching vessels, a playwright should be designing a vessel for a staged play production. A shipwright may be passionate about what he does but if he isn't ruled by the most basic principles of what it takes to put together a seaworthy craft, he's literally sunk.

Can you effectively design a ship if you've never built one?

It's a valuable investment to become involved in writers' groups, to read plays and to study the principles of playwriting. However, if you want to create a truly stage-worthy play, it requires much more.

I'm convinced that the best training for an aspiring playwright can be found in the theatre itself. Audition for plays. If you can't land a role or feel that you're not wired for that kind of involvement, volunteer for any job that's available and observe. There's perhaps no better training for a playwright than serving as a prompter for a production. As a prompter, you become intimate with the script and how it is affects the creation of theatre.

Continual observation of the rehearsal process will get you close to the complete art of theatre. You truly learn about a play's structure by seeing a director endeavor to put it on the stage. The kinds of things that a playwright needs to communicate to set, costume and lighting designers by the way they write can become a revelation through the simple act of witnessing a production come together. You will learn how actors respond to a script by being in the house and watching them revel in and struggle with what's on the page. These experiences will reveal the building blocks of a good play in a way that can't be learned in solitude.

If you want to be a shipwright, begin by learning how seaworthy ships are built. If you want to be a playwright, you begin by learning how a stage-worthy play is built.

Inside a Director's Head
by Steve Cleberg

It's a confounding truth that the well written plays are not always the plays that are getting produced. If they were, then theatre companies would stage nothing but the canons of such playwrights as Shakespeare, Moliere, Ibsen and other masters. There would be no need for new playwrights.

Every year my theatre produces an evening of short plays, entitled Sketches!, for which we receive over 200 submissions a year. I'll be honest; I often don't finish reading a play that I begin. The reason for this is rarely a value judgement.

When a director reads a play for possible production the process is inherently "unfair." The playwright should embrace this condition. Think about it; do you really want a director to spend the time and energy it takes to produce your play if he or she isn't passionate about it?

The act of reading a play for possible production is similar to casting a play. It is, and should be, highly subjective. A director looking for a play to produce is looking for something very specific. The specifics are different for every director and they will likely change from season to season. However, there are a few questions that run through my head when I read a play for possible production. Below are three questions that I believe every director is asking as they read a submitted play.

"How will my audience respond to this play?"

If I believe that my audience will benefit, either from the message or the entertainment value of the work, I will continue reading. At times, I come across a different type of play which may help build my audience. Usually, I can tell if the play I'm reading fits this particular requirement within a page or two.

"Do I have the talent to fill these roles?"

My talent pool is smaller than you will find in an urban area. I hold open auditions but I have a pretty good idea of who will show up. I always leave room for new talent but I'm not going to take a chance that an actor who fits a specific type of character will show up at auditions. Sometimes I may set a script aside based on the description of the characters.

"Is this play something with which I want to spend the next six to eight weeks?"

There is a lot of "eye-rolling" that goes on when directors read plays. This occurs when inevitable clichés or over-cleverness arise. I tend to do my eye-rolling with more levity than other directors because I was once a young playwright who, no doubt, caused my fair share of directors to roll their eyes. I could make a list of common offenders but they are different for every director. A character or situation that makes me squeamish may be appealing to another.

Bottom line: Write what strikes you as true, not what you think will appeal to someone else. As I tell actors who are auditioning, don't hesitate to stand up and be counted because you're afraid you may not fit a role in the play. You may not have the precise quality that a director is looking for in one play but that quality may work perfectly for the next play he produces. Not only that, the act of auditioning is the act of performing and there's no better experience for an actor.

In the same way, there is much to be gained by submitting your work to as many directors as possible, no matter how many times your play is not picked up. For

"Sketches!" we have often passed over a play one year only to discover that it satisfies all of the "director's questions" for a subsequent season.

Lesson learned: keep creating!

Kentucky Playwrights Workshop, Inc.

Membership year September 1 – August 31 annually
Dues: $35 for Regular Membership; $25 for Associate Membership; $15 Students

Regular Membership: open to residents of Kentucky. May enter the Kentucky New Play Series short play contest which is only open to KPW members. Discounts on KPW conferences and programs. Discount on advertising in Kentucky Theatre Yearbook and possible free bio in Kentucky Playwrights Corner. Free copy of Kentucky Theatre Yearbook. No pro-rated dues.

Associate Membership: open to Kentucky playwrights wherever they live. Discounts on KPW conferences and programs; discounted bio in Kentucky Playwrights Corner and discount on the regular price of Kentucky Theatre Yearbook. No pro-rated dues.

Student Membership: open to students of Kentucky high schools and colleges or universities, and of graduates of Kentucky colleges or universities, and enrollees in a graduate program in playwriting at Spalding University or in a contiguous state. May enter the Kentucky New Play Series short play contest which is only open to KPW regular and student members. Discounts on KPW conferences and programs. Free copy of Kentucky Theatre Yearbook. No pro-rated dues.

For more information about KPW visit
Kentucky Playwrights Workshop, Inc. on Facebook

Send dues to KPW, PO Box 59, Corinth, KY 41010

Dividing Adam's Ashes
by A. K. Forbes

Editor's Note: *Dividing Adam's Ashes* premiered at KTA Community Theatre Festival directed by Patrick Downey It featured Steve Myers as Chief, Nathan Henegar as Ducky and Joe Doscher as Martin.

Regarding Royalties: Amateurs and professionals are hereby notified that the version of *Dividing Adam's Ashes* appearing in this book is a literary version only. Appearance in this book does not give readers the right to perform the play without the express consent of the author and the payment of appropriate royalties. Information about how to secure performance rights to this play are elsewhere in this book.

Synopsis: Three men debate the fate of a friend's ashes, sparking conversation and confrontation over marriage, mistakes and Moses.

CHARACTERS
CHIEF – struggling with matters of faith and mortality
DUCKY – the easygoing clown; uses humor to avoid
MARTIN – distracted; trying to save his marriage

SETTING
A patio outside the clubhouse of a golf course

TIME
The present

AT RISE: Three men stand on the patio outside a golf course clubhouse, gathered around an urn.

CHIEF: So. How are we going to do this?

DUCKY: Divide it up, I guess.

CHIEF: We can't divide it up—

MARTIN: You can't divide a person up.

DUCKY: Pretty sure you can. *(Looks from the others.)* I'm not saying we <u>should</u>. Just saying we can. He's not like one giant chunk.

CHIEF: Jesus. He was a person, Ducky.

DUCKY: Right. And now he's a bunch of little powdery, fossil-y… pieces of...

MARTIN: We could set a schedule.

CHIEF: A schedule for Adam's ashes? Like I get him on weekends with a full moon and you get him after hockey season?

DUCKY: I call dibs on March Madness! He always won the pool.

CHIEF: We're not scheduling him. It's too— it's stupid. We're not going to do it that way.

MARTIN: You got a better idea, Chief? *(To Ducky:)* And no. We are not dividing him up.

DUCKY: Crazy ass thing to put in a will, though. 'I bequeath my cremains to my good friends, Martin, Chief and Ducky.'

MARTIN: 'Ducky, AKA Donald.' Donald Ducky.

DUCKY: Had no idea he knew my real name.

MARTIN: <u>No one</u> knew your real name. Until that unfortunate moment.

CHIEF *(overlapping)*: Adam's sister snorted—

DUCKY: Not my fault.

CHIEF: —at her own brother's funeral service.

MARTIN: It wasn't a funeral service, it was a reading of the—

CHIEF: She snorted!

DUCKY: Everybody calls <u>you</u> Chief. Why isn't <u>that</u> funny?

CHIEF: Because my real name isn't Knock-a-homa.

MARTIN: It's weird, isn't it? This is what's left of Adam. <u>This</u>! A freaking vase.

DUCKY: It's kind of cool. Arty.

CHIEF: For a vase, maybe. Not for a person. Not for Adam.

MARTIN: Beats being stuffed underground to rot.

DUCKY *(sings)*: The worms go in, the worms go out, go in your stomach and—

MARTIN: Can we focus, here? I have dinner plans with Katie.

DUCKY: Dinner plans? I thought that was the one great thing about having a wife. No need for dinner plans. I thought you could just count on, you know, having dinner.

MARTIN: We have date nights now. Our therapist recommended it.

DUCKY: That's cool.

MARTIN: Sure it is. *(A pause. CHIEF examines the urn.)*

CHIEF: You think this is all there is?

DUCKY: Holy guacamole. Did you spill some Adam?

CHIEF: Don't be a—It's sealed. We didn't 'spill some Adam.' I'm talking about life, dufus.

DUCKY: Oh. I hope this is all there is.

CHIEF: And why in the name of all that is holy, would you hope something like that?

DUCKY: Doesn't sound like a good time.

CHIEF: What doesn't sound like a good time?

DUCKY: Eternity. Clouds and harps. Moses.

CHIEF: That's your concept of an afterlife? Clouds and fucking harps?

MARTIN *(amused)*: And Moses.

DUCKY: I don't believe all that crap. I'm not a dumb ass.

MARTIN: Moses? Seriously?

DUCKY: The guy, the dude. In all the pictures. White robes, long white beard. Magical superpower in his finger.

MARTIN: You mean God?

DUCKY: No, the white-haired dude.

MARTIN: That's God, Ducky.

DUCKY: What? I thought it was Moses.

MARTIN: Moses holds the tablets. Divides the Red Sea. Turns snakes into water.

CHIEF: Well, in his defense, they do look similar.

DUCKY: Crap. How embarrassing would that be? I get to heaven and the first thing I do is call God 'Moses.' Ultimate party foul.

CHIEF: You two can't be as stupid as you sound right now.

DUCKY: Hey, <u>I'm</u> not the one who believes.

MARTIN *(reciting)*: Energy can neither be created nor destroyed.

DUCKY: That don't mean the white-haired dude is real, Marty.

MARTIN: The white haired dude <u>isn't</u> real. There is no 'dude,' dude.

CHIEF: Then let's just dump his ashes in the garbage, who cares?

MARTIN: Christ. Settle down, Chief. I'm not saying there's nothing…necessarily. And either way, you know, we need to…respect.

DUCKY *(sings)*: R E S P E C T, find out what it means to me—

CHIEF: When he decided to will his ashes to us, he was alive. And probably joking. Or high. Or suffering from a serious case of chemo brain. Now he's dead, so… Plus, we can 'respect' him without his ashes. We can respect him every time we slice on the fourteenth fairway.

DUCKY: Yeah, or every time we mess around with each other's girlfriends.

(Stunned silence.)

MARTIN: <u>Adam</u> moved out. It was Adam who—Chelsea was alone and I was—

DUCKY: Married!

MARTIN: Adam wasn't even sick yet.

DUCKY: So it's okay as long as no one's dying of cancer?

CHIEF: It was a mistake, Ducky. Jesus. Everyone knows that. Let's not—Let's just—

MARTIN: If it's any consolation to you, it probably destroyed my marriage.

DUCKY: I could understand it if Adam wasn't your friend. If Chelsea was just some girl.

MARTIN: I know. I suck. I'm going to hell. Just ask Katie.

DUCKY: Then maybe there <u>is</u> a god.

CHIEF: C'mon, Ducky.

(An uncomfortable silence.)

DUCKY: You ever watch "Long Island Medium?" It's about some lady. She talks to the dead. I think she's from Long Island.

CHIEF: Good job there, Ducky.

DUCKY: She says to look for signs. Like if a butterfly lands on your shoulder that might be Adam saying hello.

MARTIN: A mother effing butterfly. Jesus.

DUCKY: Not necessarily a butterfly. It can be anything. It can be a lot of things. *(Martin's phone rings.)* It can be a phone.

MARTIN: It's Katie.

CHIEF: Go ahead, Marty.

MARTIN: No, I'll—It's fine. She'll just have to understand, that's all. It's not every day you deal with your friend's ashes.

DUCKY: Turn your phone off. Tell her your battery went dead.

MARTIN: That kind of thinking, Ducky, is exactly why you're still single.

DUCKY: That and knowing my limitations.

(Martin turns off his phone and puts it in his pocket.)

CHIEF: The butterfly thing—signs, whatever...Do you think—? I got this voice mail yesterday, an old voice mail, somehow it got re-sent... It was a message from Adam.

DUCKY: Freaky deekie do.

CHIEF: He said, 'I need your help, man. Call me.' Seemed so real. Like he was still alive somewhere.

MARTIN: I was with him at the hospital. Trust me. He's dead.

CHIEF: What's that supposed to mean?

MARTIN: It just means I saw him die.

CHIEF *(Sarcastic)*: Oh, that's all? All hail the prodigal friend, Martin Frasier.

MARTIN: Don't be a douche—

CHIEF: I was in Colorado. On the trip Ellie and I had planned since seventh grade. In the mountains, without cell service and he wasn't supposed to die yet. He was supposed to live until… If anyone should have been with him, it should have been me.

DUCKY: Did you try calling him back?

MARTIN: Oh my God, how stupid can you be—

CHIEF: Yeah, I called him. Of course I called him.

DUCKY: And?

CHIEF: Moses answered. What the hell do you think?

DUCKY: Could be a sign.

MARTIN: If it's a sign, it doesn't sound good. Doesn't sound like he made it to the light.

CHIEF: Still. I have 97 saved messages. And <u>that's</u> the one that re-sends itself.

DUCKY: Too bad it wasn't that sext you got from Maria Connolly after the reunion.

MARTIN: You don't save that kind of shit, Ducky. Not if you want to stay married.

DUCKY *(Feigning surprise)*: What are you saying? Your wife goes through your phone messages?

CHIEF: Ellie doesn't.

DUCKY: Ellie doesn't need to.

CHIEF: For God's sake, Ducky. Let it go.

MARTIN: Adam left. Adam left Chelsea, not the other way around. What part of that do you not get? And it's ancient history. I'm putting effort into—I'm trying to stay married.

DUCKY: <u>That's</u> the part I don't get!

MARTIN: What? That I'm trying?

DUCKY: No. That Katie took you back.

CHIEF: Let's just focus on what we came here for. Adam's ashes. What's left of our friend.

MARTIN: Katie wants to stay married.

DUCKY: What a joke.

CHIEF: What about the golf course? Make this the final resting place of our fearsome foursome. Maybe the rough on the fourteenth fairway.

DUCKY: The banana ball takes a final bow.

CHIEF: I don't think he ever <u>didn't</u> slice on the fourteenth.

DUCKY: Maybe that's what Adam meant. He needs help with his golf game on the other side.

MARTIN: Yeah. That, or harp lessons.

CHIEF: Maybe he's different now. Transformed.

DUCKY: Oh, he's transformed, all right. He's a bunch of powdery, fossil-y pieces of junk inside a fricking vase.

MARTIN: Inspiring eulogy, Reverend Donald.

DUCKY: Can I have the vase?

CHIEF: You want to keep the urn?

DUCKY: I like it. It's arty.

MARTIN: Since when do you like art?

DUCKY: Since some girl told me I need more art crap in my apartment.

MARTIN: Then by all means, sure. Keep it.

CHIEF: Let's just do this. Let's just do this and then we can all go our separate ways.

MARTIN: Sounds awesome.

DUCKY: Wait a sec... Hold on a sec. Did you see the design? Did you really look at it? On the side of the urn.

CHIEF: I'll be damned. Is that—?

MARTIN: No shit.

DUCKY: A mother effing butterfly.

(CHIEF looks to the heavens, MARTIN pulls out his cell phone, and DUCKY studies the urn.)

Lights fade to black.

Curtain

(End of Play)

SUNNY SIDE: A Ten-Minute Comedy for Two Actors
by Philip Paradis

Editor's Note: *Sunny Side* premiered at the Kentucky State Fair as part of the 2014 Kentucky New Play Series; it was co-produced by Kentucky Playwrights Workshop, Inc. and Artist Asylum Theatre of Elizabethtown, KY, directed by Kristi Johnson, featuring Raynell Rigney as Dolly Brady and Scott Belcher as Seamus O'Malley. It was performed in 2015 at Manhattan Repertory Theatre, New York, NY.

Regarding Royalties: Amateurs and professionals are hereby notified that the version of *Sunny Side* appearing in this book is a literary version only. Appearance in this book does not give readers the right to perform the play without the express consent of the author and the payment of appropriate royalties. To arrange licensing rights, contact the author at: phil.paradis@fuse.net or (859)653-6344.

Synopsis: An old man waves to an old woman he sees daily in the park. The retired Irishman and distrusting widow meet.

TIME: Summer afternoon.

PLACE: City street.

SET: Park bench.

CHARACTERS:
MAN (Seamus O'Malley) 77, Irish, retired widower
WOMAN (Dolly Brady) 88, widow

AT RISE: MAN with a cane is seated on a park bench at center stage. WOMAN enters and approaches. The MAN looks at the WOMAN and gives her a modest little wave. WOMAN passes by him, then stops and turns.

WOMAN: Why you do that? Huh?

MAN: I waved. Hullo.

WOMAN: Why? Why do you do that? Why do you always wave at me? I don't know you.

MAN: I see you walking every day.

WOMAN: You wave at me. But I don't know you. You don't know me.

MAN: Good day. *(He rises and begins walking away.)*

WOMAN: Is it?

MAN: I was just wishing it to you.

WOMAN: What?

MAN: A good day.

WOMAN: See what good wishin' will do ya!

MAN: I say... I wished you "a good day." *(turns and walks away)* Hmph.

WOMAN: Wishin' won't make it so—now, will it?

MAN *(turning to face her)*: Good afternoon. Is that better?

WOMAN: Better than what?

MAN: "Good day."

WOMAN: Startin' that again, are you? You have a one track mind. You men are all alike... You only think about one thing. Maybe two.

MAN *(walking toward her)*: Ha-ha. Oh, no. I'm not like that. I'm 77 years old...How old are you?

WOMAN: I'm 88.

MAN: Nooo. I don't believe it.
(overlapping)

WOMAN: I am. I was born in 1927. October 20, 1927. The same year that Babe Ruth hit 60 home runs!
(overlapping)

MAN: Is that so? You don't look 88.

WOMAN: I don't feel 88. I feel good.

MAN: *(looking her up and down)*: You look more like a ... seventy-eight.

WOMAN: Oh, thank you. I feel much younger than my years. *(sits on the bench)* How much younger I won't say.
MAN: Age is a state of mind, they say. *(sits at other end of bench)* I find it's true in my own case.

WOMAN: How old did you say you were?

MAN: Seventy-seven.

WOMAN: You don't look 77.

MAN: Why thank you.

WOMAN: Maybe, seventy-five. But not seventy-seven.

MAN: Well now, I'll take that as a compliment.

WOMAN: Well, it's meant as a compliment. *(Pause)* I don't know why I'm talking to you—I never talk to strangers.

MAN: Is that what your ma told you?

WOMAN: That's right. 'Never talk to strangers.'

MAN: I might be 'the bogeyman,' or...Jack the Ripper.

WOMAN: Well I don't know. You might be up to no good.

MAN: I could be a mad man.

WOMAN: Or a criminal.
MAN: I may be a stockbroker... or worse, a banker!

WOMAN: You could be...a child molester!
MAN: A politician ... or—a lawyer.

WOMAN: You may be. *(Beat)*

MAN *(quietly) (Pause)*: I might be lonely... and wishin' nothing more than t' pass the time of day. With a lovely lady I chance to meet on this very street...on this glorious summer afternoon.

WOMAN: Well now. Aren't you the charmer?

MAN: That tune I like better. *(Pause)* Dear Lady, allow me to introduce myself. *(standing)* I'm Seamus O'Malley, at your service.

>   *(MAN attempts a deep bow but can only manage halfway.)*

WOMAN: Ohh... *(extends her hand as if to shake)* Mrs. Brady. *(Pause)* My friends call me 'Dolly.'

MAN: Well, Mrs. Brady. I'll hope that one fine day you'll count me among your lucky friends. *(HE takes her hand and bends to kiss it.)*

WOMAN *(coyly, withdrawing her hand)*: Ha. That depends.

MAN: *(Pause)* Tell me, Mrs. Brady. Why does Mr. Brady leave his lovely Mrs. to walk unescorted these mean streets and public thoroughfares?

WOMAN: Mr. Brady left us for his heavenly reward—twenty-two years, December.

MAN: I'm so sorry t'hear that, Mrs. Brady. My dear wife of forty years is ten years gone.

WOMAN: I'm sorry to hear that.

MAN: I still miss her. Every day. *(Pause)* How long were you married?

WOMAN: Forty-two years.

MAN: Oh, that's a long time.

WOMAN: I have three great-great grandchildren, 5 great-grandchildren, 8 grandchildren, two sons and a daughter.

MAN: Congratulations! That quite a family you have.

WOMAN: Why, thank you, Mr. O'Malley. I love them all. I just can't remember all of their names! *(Pause)* You have any family?

MAN: I've a daughter and son and eight grandchildren... and two great-grandchildren.

WOMAN: You have quite a family too. Forgive me, I am so out of practice talking to a gentleman. One does get a bit full of being alone without another one to talk to. I don't get out much.

MAN: Oh, no?
WOMAN: My back goes out all the time. In fact my back goes out more than I do.

MAN: Ha! A pity. The years can be so cruel. I have diabetes.

WOMAN: I have a heart condition.

MAN: High blood pressure.

WOMAN: Palpitations.

MAN: Sci-at-ica.

WOMAN: Arthur-itis. *(Pause)* How many pills do you take? I bet I take more than you.

MAN: Let's see... in morning 4, for lunch 3, at dinner 3, then bedtime 2... that's 12... I take 12.

WOMAN: I take 17... a day.

MAN *(chuckling)*: Then you win. *(Pause)* Well now, my dear Mrs. Brady, before the dark clouds roll in, would you care to take in some sun?

WOMAN: Call me "Dolly."

> *(MAN rises from the bench and offers his arm to her. WOMAN rises and takes his arm.)*

MAN: Very well then. Why of course, Dolly.

WOMAN: Stay on the sidewalk now.

> *(They walk arm-in-arm, slowly and carefully.)*

MAN: I only walk on cement or blacktop.

WOMAN: Good. The grass is too uneven.

MAN: Absolutely treacherous. *(Pause)* Hang on... hold on tight. Now don't worry, if you fall, I got you.

WOMAN: Okay. But... what if... you fall?

MAN: You'll catch me.

WOMAN: Oh no, I'm not strong enough.

(They stop. MAN turns to her.)

MAN: Then... we'll... fall together. Alright now... hang on. Here... we go.

(They resume walking slowly and EXIT.)

Curtain

(End of Play)

The Kentucky New Plays Census 2014 and 2015
by Bill McCann, Jr.

Abstract

On the pages that follow, listed alphabetically by playwright, is a compilation of new works given readings or performances in Kentucky, and new works by Kentucky playwrights given readings or performances outside Kentucky, during the calendar years 2014 and 2015. The information in this section of the *Kentucky Theatre Yearbook 2016* was compiled from back issues of *The Dramatist*, inquiries made online via Facebook pages such as The Official Playwrights of Facebook, personal knowledge, newspaper articles, and information solicited from or provided by playwrights and theatres.

This section is divided into two parts; in the first is a listing of plays given readings or performances listed by title and playwright with information about where the play was read or performed. Plays listed here may have had as few as one performance/reading. No distinction is made between 10-minute, one-act and full-length scripts.

The second part of this section lists the theatres/venues at which plays were given readings or performed during calendar years 2014 and 2015. Information in this section focuses on the theatre/venue and details/contact information for the theatre. Listings of plays and playwrights below the theatres only list the plays and playwrights; for more complete information about each play refer to the playwright entries.

Part One:
Plays Given Readings or Performances

Productions in Kentucky by Kentucky Playwrights

Inedicabilis, created by Kiefer Adkins and Sam O'Mara, 2014 New Works Festival, Western Kentucky University, Department of Theatre and Dance, Bowling Green, KY

The Big Sandy River Plays (Part I: Feud; Part II: Firebrand; Part III: Fresh Water) by Michael Ross Albert, Jenny Wiley Theatre, Pikeville/Prestonsburg, KY (Commissioned by the theatre) (Plays written and performed over the years 2012-2015)

Jim Thorpe—All American, written and performed by Chris Anger, Walden Theatre's Slant Culture Theatre Festival, Louisville, KY

Untitled by Rachel Asher, 2015 New Play Festival, J.B. Sowards Theatre, Ashland Community & Technical College, Ashland, KY

Carry On by Trish Ayers, Berea College Theatre, Berea, KY

Louisville Championship Arm Wrestling: WRIST IN PEACE (sic), devised by Baby Horse Theatre Company, Walden Theatre's Slant Culture Theatre Festival, Louisville, KY

Oedipus Rex: The Original MF, created by the Bard's Town Theatre, Walden Theatre's Slant Culture Theatre Festival, Louisville, KY

Until Death by Malynda Brooke Barker, 2014 New Play Festival, J.B. Sowards Theatre, Ashland Community & Technical College, Ashland, KY

Little Girl Lost by Malynda Brook Barker, 2015 New Play Festival, J.B. Sowards Theatre, Ashland Community & Technical College, Ashland, KY

Armistice by Isaac Barnes, 2014 New Works Festival, Western Kentucky University, Department of Theatre and Dance, Bowling Green, KY

Bull by Mark Bartlett, Walden Theatre's Slant Culture Theatre Festival, Louisville, KY

Agatha, written and performed by Melinda Beck, Walden Theatre's Slant Culture Theatre Festival, Louisville, KY

The Rearview Mirror by Kristen Bell, 2015 New Voices Young Playwrights Festival, Actors Theatre of Louisville, Louisville, KY

Meeting for the First Time by Lindsey Blankenship, 2015 New Play Festival, J.B. Sowards Theatre, Ashland Community & Technical College, Ashland, KY

Rose Upon a White Gait by Tammy Brady, 4th Annual Kentucky New Play Series, Kentucky Playwrights Workshop, Corinth, KY, performed at the Kentucky State Fair, Louisville, KY

Luna by Lena Buechler, 2014 New Works Festival, Western Kentucky University, Department of Theatre and Dance, Bowling Green, KY

Keeping Traditions by Sarah Diamond Burroway, ACTC Student Showcase, Ashland Community & Technical College, Ashland, KY

It's Just a Box by Sarah Diamond Burroway (People's Choice Best Play), 2015 New Play Festival, J.B. Sowards Theatre, Ashland Community & Technical College, Ashland, KY

It's Just a Box- A One-Act Play of Short Monologues by Sarah Diamond Burroway, Ten-Tucky Festival of Ten-Minute Plays, The Bard's Town Theatre, Louisville, KY

It's Just a Box- A One-Act Play of Short Monologues by Sarah Diamond Burroway, Ashland Community and Technical College Theatre, 2015 New Works Festival, Ashland, KY

To the Woman at Food Fair Who Screamed at Her Child by Sarah Diamond Burroway, 2015 New Play Festival, J.B. Sowards Theatre, Ashland Community & Technical College, Ashland, KY

Wash Day (or Perspectives on Laundry)- a short, comedic play by Sarah Diamond Burroway, 4th Annual Kentucky New Play Series, Kentucky Playwrights Workshop, Corinth, KY, performed at the Kentucky State Fair, Louisville, KY

Walking Across Egypt by Catherine Bush (adapted from the novel by Clyde Edgerton), Pioneer Playhouse, Danville, KY

The Choice by Jillian Carpenter, Kohn Theatre, University of the Cumberlands, Williamsburg, KY

Toy Fight by Kristen Carroll, 2015 New Play Festival, J.B. Sowards Theatre, Ashland Community & Technical College, Ashland, KY

6,600 Volts by Robyn Carroll, The Tens: An Evening of 10-minute Plays, Actors Theatre of Louisville, Louisville, KY

What Would Jesus Pack? by Ross Carter, Studio Players, Lexington, KY

Reindeer by Richard Cavendish, 3rd Annual Kentucky New Play Series, Artist Asylum Theatre, Elizabethtown, performed at the Kentucky State Fair, Louisville, KY

The Two Villages by Richard Cavendish, commissioned by Kentucky Playwrights Workshop, produced by Artist Asylum Theatre, Elizabethtown, KY, at The Bard's Town Theatre, Louisville, KY

Saint Bob by Tad Chitwood, 8th Finnigan's Festival of Funky Fresh Fun, produced by The Derby City Playwrights, The Bard's Town, Louisville, KY

The Maids by Jean Genet, adapted by Tad Chitwood, Walden Theatre's Slant Culture Theatre Festival, produced by Savage Rose Classical Theatre Company, Louisville, KY

Cody Clark: A Different Way of Thinking, written and performed by Cody Clark, Walden Theatre's Slant Culture Theatre Festival, Louisville, KY

And in the Silence Penguins Come by David Clark, 8th Finnigan's Festival of Funky Fresh Fun, produced by The Derby City Playwrights, The Bard's Town, Louisville, KY

Tin Pan Alley Tavern (a musical), by Steve Cleberg, Somerset Community College Theatre, Somerset, KY

Two Loves and a River by Don Coffey, The Capital City Museum, Frankfort, KY

The Torpedo Room by Benjamin Collins, 2015 New Voices Young Playwrights Festival, Actors Theatre of Louisville, Louisville, KY

Glass Carousel by Jacob Craigo-Snell, Young Playwrights Festival, 2015, Walden Theatre and Blue Apple Players, Louisville, KY

Earl by Chase Davaney, 2014 New Play Festival, J.B. Sowards Theatre, Ashland Community & Technical College, Ashland, KY

Days Gone By by Will DeVary, Young Playwrights Festival, 2015, Walden Theatre and Blue Apple Players, Louisville, KY

Want You Back by Kora Duvall, Young Playwrights Festival, 2015, Walden Theatre and Blue Apple Players, Louisville, KY

#NotAllMen by Ruthie Dworkin, Young Playwrights Festival, 2015, Walden Theatre and Blue Apple Players, Louisville, KY

Strange Things Happen by Chelsea G. Fannin (People's Choice Best Play), 2014 New Play Festival, J.B. Sowards Theatre, Ashland Community & Technical College, Ashland, KY

Angels My Father Sent by Erika Finley, Lindsey Wilson College, V.P. Henry Auditorium, Columbia, KY

Marilyn by Isiah Fish, 2014 New Works Festival, Western Kentucky University, Department of Theatre and Dance, Bowling Green, KY

Stay, written and performed by Isiah Fish, 2014 New Works Festival, Western Kentucky University, Department of Theatre and Dance, Bowling Green, KY

The Faculty Lounge by Teri Foltz, Carnegie Arts Center, Covington, KY

The Off Chance by Teri Foltz, Short Play Lab, Midtown International Theatre Festival, New York, NY
Flight Path by A.K. Forbes, 4th Annual Kentucky New Play Series, Kentucky Playwrights Workshop, Corinth, KY, performed at the Kentucky State Fair, Louisville, KY

A Curiosity Quilt by Nancy Gall-Clayton, 3rd Annual Kentucky New Play Series, Artist Asylum Theatre, Elizabethtown, KY, performed at the Kentucky State Fair, Louisville, KY
A Deal by Nancy Gall-Clayton, 8th Finnigan's Festival of Funky Fresh Fun, produced by The Derby City Playwrights, The Bard's Town Theatre, Louisville, KY
A Trip to Eden by Nancy Gall-Clayton, The Bard's Town Theatre, Louisville, KY

The Landscape of Tomorrow by Nancy Gall-Clayton, commissioned by Kentucky Playwrights Workshop, produced by Artist Asylum Theatre, Elizabethtown, KY, The Bard's Town Theatre, Louisville, KY
Levels of Living by Nancy Gall-Clayton, The Bard's Town Theatre, Louisville, KY
Lightening Up by Nancy Gall-Clayton, Derby City Playwrights, The Bard's Town, Louisville, KY
My Turquoise Sock by Nancy Gall-Clayton, Shape & Flow Writing Instruction, The Bard's Town Theatre, Louisville, KY
Shakespeare & Thee by Nancy Gall-Clayton, Shape & Flow Writing Instruction, Mellwood Arts & Entertainment Center, Louisville, KY

The Poet From Pikeville by Nancy Gall-Clayton, Berea College Theatre, Berea, KY

The Poet From Pikeville (radio play version) by Nancy Gall-Clayton, hosted by Trish Ayers, Berea, KY

The Fish in the Dumpster by Nancy Gall-Clayton, Jelkyl Drama Center, Berea College, Berea, KY

Zimy and Zog Visit Earth by Nancy Gall-Clayton, Finigan's 7th Annual Festival of Funky Fresh Fun, The Bard's Town, Louisville, KY

3 x 10: Betty & Bob's B & B; Hair Today; and *Mr. Fix-It Saves the Night* by Nancy Gall-Clayton, produced by Ronald R. Van Stockum, Jr., Little Colonel Playhouse, Pewee Valley, KY

Stops by Ben Gierhart, 8th Finnigan's Festival of Funky Fresh Fun, produced by The Derby City Playwrights, The Bard's Town Theatre, Louisville, KY

Looking for Mr. Right by Catherine Rhoden Goguen, Knox Central High School, Barbourville KY

Safety by Amanda Haan, 8th Finnigan's Festival of Funky Fresh Fun, produced by The Derby City Playwrights, The Bard's Town Theatre, Louisville, KY

Waiting for Bardot by Clara Harris, Readers Theatre, Somerset Community College Theatre, Somerset, KY

A Haunting in the East Wing by Katie Henning, 2015 New Voices Young Playwrights Festival, Actors Theatre of Louisville, Louisville, KY

The Wonder Team by Robby Henson, Pioneer Playhouse, Danville, KY

Looks Can Be Deceiving by Delaney Hildreth, Young Playwrights Festival, 2015, Walden Theatre and Blue Apple Players, Louisville, KY

I Hate Vampires by Jessica K. Howard, 2015 New Works Festival, J.B. Sowards Theatre, Ashland Community & Technical College, Ashland, KY

Polynomial Dysfunction by Jessica K. Howard, 2014 New Works Festival, J.B. Sowards Theatre, Ashland Community & Technical College, Ashland, KY

Remedial Lessons by Arlene Hutton, Berea College Theatre, Berea, KY

Starcrossed by Brooke Jennett & Mollie LaFavers, Shakespeare in Mind, Transylvania University Theatre, Lexington, KY

Zombie Love by Jennifer Johnson, 4th Annual Kentucky New Play Series, Kentucky Playwrights Workshop, Corinth, KY, performed at the Kentucky State Fair, Louisville, KY

Zombie Love by Jennifer Johnson, 2015 New Play Festival, J.B. Sowards Theatre, Ashland Community & Technical College, Ashland, KY

The Lesson by Eugene Ionesco, translated by Nancy Jones, Walden Theatre's Slant Culture Theatre Festival, produced by Theatre Farouche, Louisville, KY

If They Do See Thee by Jon Jory, Shakespeare in Mind, Transylvania University Theatre, Lexington, KY

Tammy and Tom by Jonathan Joy, 2014 New Play Festival, J.B. Sowards Theatre, Ashland Community & Technical College, Ashland, KY

You Better Sit Down: Tales from My Parents' Divorce, written or created by Anne Kaufman, Mathew

Maher, Caitlin Miller, Jennifer R. Morris, Janice Paran, Robbie Collier Sublet, Walden Theatre's Slant Culture Theatre Festival, produced by Eve Theatre Company, Louisville, KY

Among the Quick and the Dead by John Kelly, 2015 Summer Shorts, Theatre Workshop Owensboro, Owensboro, KY

Sausage Fest by Eli Keel, 8th Finnigan's Festival of Funky Fresh Fun, produced by The Derby City Playwrights, The Bard's Town Theatre, Louisville, KY

Finger Play (not a real title) by Basil Kreimendahl, Remix 38, 38th Humana Festival of New American Plays, Actors Theatre of Louisville, Louisville, KY

Like We Do by Basil Kreimendahl, Remix 38, 38th Humana Festival of New American Plays, Actors Theatre of Louisville, Louisville, KY

Sidewinders by Basil Kreimendahl, Looking for Lilith Theatre Company, Louisville, KY

Chipped by Becky LeCron, 8th Finnigan's Festival of Funky Fresh Fun, produced by The Derby City Playwrights, The Bard's Town Theatre, Louisville, KY

Sleepy Hollow by Harper Lee, inspired by the story by Washington Irving, The Public Theatre of Kentucky in partnership with the Western Kentucky University Department of Theatre and Dance, Bowling Green, KY

Prevailing Winds, created and produced by Looking for Lilith Theatre Company, Louisville, KY

Uncaged Desenjauladas, devised by Looking for Lilith Theatre Company, Walden Theatre's Slant Culture Theatre Festival, produced by Looking for Lilith Theatre Company, Louisville, KY

The Buddy Glim Show, created/improvised/produced by Louisville Improvisors, Walden Theatre's Slant Culture Theatre Festival, Louisville, KY

The Road through Damascus by Robert Macke, Northern Kentucky University, Department of Theatre and Dance, Highland Heights, KY

Grounded, adapted by Chelsea Marcantel (from the novel of the same name by Angela Correll), Pioneer Playhouse, Danville, KY

An Expressive Existence, created by Eric Mattingly and the Ensemble, 2014 New Works Festival, Western Kentucky University, Department of Theatre and Dance, Bowling Green, KY

This Was Racing: An Evening with Joe Palmer, by Walter May, performed at the Keeneland Library (by the author), Lexington, KY

Exercise the Cat by Tish Maynard, 2015 New Play Festival, J.B. Sowards Theatre, Ashland Community & Technical College, Ashland, KY

Silver Sleuths by Tish Maynard, 2015 New Play Festival, J.B. Sowards Theatre, Ashland Community & Technical College, Ashland, KY

My Father Thinks He's Irish by George McGee, 3rd Annual Kentucky New Play Series, Artist Asylum Theatre, Elizabethtown, performed at the Kentucky State Fair, Louisville, KY

Something Must Be Done by George McGee, commissioned by Kentucky Playwrights Workshop, produced by Artist Asylum Theatre, Elizabethtown, KY at The Bard's Town Theatre, Louisville, KY

Pirate Treasure by Geanna McGlone, 2015 New Play Festival, J.B. Sowards Theatre, Ashland Community & Technical College, Ashland, KY

Murder the Devil by Cisco Montgomery (Larry Muhammad's pen name), Cisco Montgomery Inc., Louisville, KY. Full production at The Vault 1031, Louisville, KY

Three Plays from Cisco (Radio Play, Kin Under the Skin, and ***Boomerang)*** produced by Cisco Montgomery Inc. Full production at MeX Theatre, Kentucky Center, Louisville, KY

A Starfish's World by Brooke Morrison, 2015 New Voices Young Playwrights Festival, Actors Theatre of Louisville, Louisville, KY

The Stranger and Ludlow Quinn (a serialized play) by Steve Moulds and Diana Grisanti, commissioned/produced by Theatre [502], Louisville, KY

The Wedding Guest by Steve Moulds (Commissioned by the Apprentice Company), Actors Theatre of Louisville, Louisville, KY

Buster! The Musical by Larry Muhammad, Kentucky Black Repertory Theatre, Louisville, KY; full production at Henry Clay Theatre, Louisville, KY

Double V by Larry Muhammad, produced by the Filson Historical Society, Louisville, KY. Full production at Muhammad Ali Center, Louisville, KY

You Hear Me Speak by Dare Norman, 2014 New Works Festival, Western Kentucky University, Department of Theatre and Dance, Bowling Green, KY

Kentucky October by Sam O'Mara, 2014 New Works Festival, Western Kentucky University, Department of Theatre and Dance, Bowling Green, KY

Anita Maan by Ruby Osborne, Young Playwrights Festival, 2015, Walden Theatre and Blue Apple Players, Louisville, KY

Desdemona's Heart by Jeremy Paden, Shakespeare in Mind, Transylvania University Theatre, Lexington, KY

Twisted Shakespeare I & II by Jeremy Paden, Shakespeare in Mind, Transylvania University Theatre, Lexington, KY

Sunny Side by Philip Paradis, 3rd Annual Kentucky New Play Series, Artist Asylum Theatre, Elizabethtown, KY, performed at the Kentucky State Fair, Louisville, KY

The Great Debate by Philip Paradis, Village Players Theatre, Ft. Thomas, KY

The Kitty Cat Ultimatum by Philip Paradis, Village Players Theatre, Ft. Thomas, KY

Soldier's Christmas by Philip Paradis, New Edgecliff Theatre with Actors & Playwrights Collaborative, Corbett Theatre, Northern Kentucky University, Highland Heights, KY

Sober by Miranda Parsons, 2015 New Play Festival, J.B. Sowards Theatre, Ashland Community & Technical College, Ashland, KY

Beyond Sight by Trena Penney, 2015 New Play Festival, J.B. Sowards Theatre, Ashland Community & Technical College, Ashland, KY

Who Dunnit, Darling? by Charles Edward Pogue and Larry Drake, Pioneer Playhouse, Danville, KY

Namaste by Stephanie Porter, 4th Annual Kentucky New Play Series, Kentucky Playwrights Workshop, Corinth, KY, performed at the Kentucky State Fair, Louisville, KY

Alone by Della Preston, 2015 New Play Festival, J.B. Sowards Theatre, Ashland Community & Technical College, Ashland, KY

A Kentucky Christmas, adapted for the stage by James W. Rodgers, Woodford Theatre, Versailles, KY

Little Red by Gil Rognstad, Roh's Theatre Co., Roh's Opera House, Cynthiana, KY

The Q & A by John Rooney, The Tens: An Evening of 10-minute Plays, Actors Theatre of Louisville, Louisville, KY

The Trouble with Boys by Alexx Rouse, Northern Kentucky University, Department of Theatre and Dance, Highland Heights, KY

Stan O'Donald's Retro Radio Review, devised by Rose Barn Theatre, cast and director, Rose Barn Theatre, Richmond, KY

When Grandma Davis Hit the Glass by Rebecca Ryland, 3rd Annual Kentucky New Play Series, Artist Asylum Theatre, Elizabethtown, KY, performed at the Kentucky State Fair, Louisville, KY

Jane the Plain by August Schulenberg, Walden Theatre's Slant Culture Theatre Festival, produced by Walden Theatre, Louisville, KY

Just Like Life by Doug Schutte, The Bard's Town Theatre, Louisville, KY

Chasing Ophelia by Doug Schutte, Kentucky Shakespeare Festival, Louisville, KY

The Kings of Christmas by Doug Schutte, The Bard's Town Theatre, Louisville, KY

The Flingin' Wisbees by Kallen Sebastian, 2015 New Voices Young Playwrights Festival, Actors Theatre of Louisville, Louisville, KY

Where Are You Christmas? By John Seidenberg II, Kincaid Regional Theatre, Falmouth, KY

Building Bridges by Mary Shortridge, 2014 New Works Festival, J.B. Sowards Theatre, Ashland Community & Technical College, Ashland, KY

The Gifted Tree by Mary Shortridge, 2014 New Works Festival, J.B. Sowards Theatre, Ashland Community & Technical College, Ashland, KY

Retribution by Mary Shortridge, 2014 New Works Festival, J.B. Sowards Theatre, Ashland Community & Technical College, Ashland, KY

Gogglebox Hamlet by Valerie Smith, Shakespeare in Mind, Transylvania University Theatre, Lexington, KY

Don't Leave Me Here, Okay? by Annie Stone, 2015 New Voices Young Playwrights Festival, Actors Theatre of Louisville, Louisville, KY

But is it Art? by Dudley Stone, Rose Barn Theatre, Richmond, KY

Purgatwar by Miranda Swan, 2014 New Works Festival, Western Kentucky University, Department of Theatre and Dance, Bowling Green, KY

Puzzle Piece by Elliott Talkington, 2014 New Works Festival, Western Kentucky University, Department of Theatre and Dance, Bowling Green, KY

Ton of Bricks by Think Tank Theatre, Walden Theatre's Slant Culture Theatre Festival, produced by Think Tank Theatre, Louisville, KY

Street Smarts by Lauren Titus, 2015 New Voices Young Playwrights Festival, Actors Theatre of Louisville, Louisville, KY

A Homeless Holiday by Juergen K. Tossman, Bunbury Theatre, Louisville, KY

Bonhoffer the Last Encounter by Juergen K. Tossman, Bunbury Theatre, Louisville, KY

Forgive Me it's Christmas by Juergen K. Tossman, Bunbury Theatre, Louisville, KY

Patchworked, written and performed by Becca Trimbur, 2014 New Works Festival, Western Kentucky University, Department of Theatre and Dance, Bowling Green, KY

Cruise Control by Ben Unwin, 8th Finnigan's Festival of Funky Fresh Fun, produced by The Derby City Playwrights, The Bard's Town, Louisville, KY

Sick by Huy Vo, 2015 New Voices Young Playwrights Festival, Actors Theatre of Louisville, Louisville, KY

dirty sexy derby play by Brian Walker, Louisville Repertory Theatre, Kentucky Center for the Arts, Louisville, KY

Gamers 4 Life by Brian David Walker, 8th Finnigan's Festival of Funky Fresh Fun, produced by The Derby City Playwrights, The Bard's Town, Louisville, KY

Hero Worship by Brian Walker, Ten-Tucky Festival of Ten-Minute Plays, The Bard's Town, Louisville, KY

Sorcar's Successor(s) by Brian Walker, Theatre [502], Baron Theatre, Louisville, KY

Visitation Privileges by Brian Walker, 3rd Annual Kentucky New Play Series, Artist Asylum Theatre, Elizabethtown, KY performed at the Kentucky State Fair, Louisville, KY

I Dedicate this Ride—The Life and Times of Isaac Murphy by Frank X. Walker, Breeder's Cup Festival, Lyric Theatre, Lexington, KY

The River Shore by Abigail Walker, Northern Kentucky University, Department of Theatre and Dance, Highland Heights, KY

The Sundial Enthusiast by Abigail Walker, Northern Kentucky University, Department of Theatre and Dance, Highland Heights, KY

Sex Again by Heidi Saunders Walker, Frog Pump Productions, Vault 1031, Louisville, KY

Southern Beauty by Brenda K. White, Berea College Theatre, Berea KY

American Goddess by Rachel White, 8th Finnigan's Festival of Funky Fresh Fun, produced by The Derby City Playwrights, The Bard's Town, Louisville, KY

Blizzard of '92 by Rachel White, Walden Theatre's Slant Culture Theatre Festival, produced by Marrow Street Theatre, Louisville, KY

Dante's Memory Tomb by Rachel White, Baron's Theatre, Louisville, KY

Eeenie Meany by Teresa Willis, Bunbury Theatre, Louisville, KY

The Snow Queeen (sic) by Stanton Wood, based on the Hans Christian Anderson story, Walden Theatre's Slant Culture Theatre Festival, produced by Walden Theatre, Louisville, KY

In the Closet by Bryce Woodard, 8th Finnigan's Festival of Funky Fresh Fun, produced by The Derby City Playwrights, The Bard's Town Theatre, Louisville, KY

Chivalry by Justin Wright, Shakespeare in Mind, Transylvania University Theatre, Lexington, KY

Trigger Happy by Rebecca Wright, 2015 Summer Shorts, Theatre Workshop Owensboro, Owensboro, KY

Gateway by Todd Zeigler, 8th Finnigan's Festival of Funky Fresh Fun, produced by The Derby City Playwrights, The Bard's Town, Louisville, KY

Kentucky Playwrights with Productions Outside Kentucky

Canada

The Anesthetic was Psalms by Nancy Gall-Clayton, Hespeler Library, Cambridge, Ontario, Canada
May I Have Your Attention, Please? By Catherine Rhoden Goguen, La Crete Public School, La Crete, Alberta, Canada
May I Have Your Attention, Please? By Catherine Rhoden Goguen, George McDougall High School, Airdrie, Alberta, Canada

United States

Painting the Egress by Trish Ayers, North Park Vaudeville and Candy Shop, San Diego, CA
Straight Out of the Closet by Trish Ayers, North Park Vaudeville and Candy Shop, San Diego, CA

The Bridges of Madison County, music & lyrics by Jason Robert Brown, book by Marsha Norman, Gerald Schoenfeld Theatre, New York, NY
Keeping Traditions by Sarah Diamond Burroway, 4th Annual Hard Candy Christmas Festival, Charles Stewart Howard Playhouse, Woodland Hills, CA
To the Woman at Food Fair Who Screamed at Her Child- a monologue by Sarah Diamond Burroway, produced by V-Day/4th Universalist Society as part of Women's Voices, a curated preshow with *I am an Emotional Creature* by Eve Ensler, Central Park West, New York, NY

Signing Off- a monologue by Sarah Diamond Burroway, The 6th Annual Women of Appalachia's "Women Speak" event, April 10, 2015 at Arts/West, Athens, OH

Signing Off- a monologue by Sarah Diamond Burroway, The 6th Annual Women of Appalachia's "Women Speak" event, May 29, 2015 at PVG Artisans, Chillicothe, OH

Interrogation by James Colgan, Lucky Penny Productions, Napa, CA

Rosencrantz and Guildenstern are Not Dead by Fredric DeJaco, Playfest 2015, South of Broadway Theater, Charleston, SC

Liz's Circus Story by Liz Fentress, Sun City Players Community Theatre, Sun City, AZ

Magpie by Teri Foltz, North Park Vaudeville Theater, San Diego, CA

Double Entrée by Nancy Gall-Clayton, Gi60 International One Minute Play Festival, Brooklyn College, NY

In the Pumpkin Patch by Nancy Gall-Clayton, The Drilling Company, New York, NY

The Palmetto Family by Nancy Gall-Clayton, Pandora Theatre's Vox Feminia V: Mom's the Word, located at The Company Onstage Theatre, Houston, TX

Shakespeare and Thee by Nancy Gall-Clayton, "Shorts" Philadelphia Modern Orthodox High School, Philadelphia, PA

Looking for Mr. Right by Catherine Rhoden Goguen, Palo Verde Theatre Department, Las Vegas, NV
Looking for Mr. Right by Catherine Rhoden Goguen, Osawatomie High School Osawatomie KS
Looking for Mr. Right by Catherine Rhoden Goguen, Bovina High School, Bovina TX
Looking for Mr. Right by Catherine Rhoden Goguen, Great Mills High School, Great Mills, MD
May I Have Your Attention, Please? by Catherine Rhoden Goguen, Westchester Enriched Sciences Magnets, Los Angeles, CA
May I Have Your Attention, Please? by Catherine Rhoden Goguen, Arden Club Theatre, Wilmington, DE
May I Have Your Attention, Please? by Catherine Rhoden Goguen, Pillsbury Baptist College, Owatonna, MN
May I Have Your Attention, Please? by Catherine Rhoden Goguen, Prairie High School, Petersburg, ND
May I Have Your Attention, Please? by Catherine Rhoden Goguen, Brecksville Theatre on the Square, Brecksville, OH
May I Have Your Attention, Please? by Catherine Rhoden Goguen, Abbeville Opera House, Abbeville, SC
May I Have Your Attention, Please? by Catherine Rhoden Goguen, Cambridge Academy, Greenwood, SC
May I Have Your Attention, Please? by Catherine Rhoden Goguen, Ripon High School, Ripon, WI

Kissed the Girls and Made Them Cry by Arlene Hutton, Playhouse on Park, West Hartford, CT

The Maids by Jean Genet, translated by Nancy C. Jones, La Mama Experimental Theatre, New York, NY

This Was Racing: An Evening with Joe Palmer by Walter May (performed by the author), National Museum of Racing and Hall of Fame, Saratoga Springs, NY

Aiden's Gift by Elizabeth Shear Orendorff, Silverthorne Theatre Company, Greenfield, MA
Have a Nice Day by Elizabeth Shear Orendorff, North Park Vaudeville & Candy Shoppe, San Diego, CA
The Search for Tinker Doyle by Elizabeth Shear Orendorff, Tri-County Players, Sharonville Fine Arts Center, Sharonville, OH

Breaking Gulf News by Phil Paradis, Manhattan Repertory Theatre, New York, NY
Daddy's Little Girl by Philip Paradis, Manhattan Repertory Theatre, New York, NY
God is a Ford Man by Philip Paradis, Manhattan Repertory Theatre, New York, NY
The Great Debate by Philip Paradis, North Park Playwright Festival, San Diego, CA
The Holey Swiss Duet by Philip Paradis, Manhattan Repertory Theatre
The Powder Puff Heist by Philip Paradis, Manhattan Repertory Theatre, New York, NY
Racquetball by Philip Paradis, The producers Club, New York, NY
Sunny Side by Philip Paradis, Manhattan Repertory Theatre, New York, NY
Sunny Side by Philip Paradis, Mirror Theatre, North Hollywood, CA
A Flea in her Ear adapted by Charles Edward Pogue, Center Stage, Greenville, SC

And I and Silence by Naomi Wallace, Signature Theatre Company, New York, NY
The Liquid Plain by Naomi Wallace, Signature Theatre Company, New York, NY
Night is a Room by Naomi Wallace, Alice Griffin Jewel Box Theatre New York, NY
Southern Beauty by Brenda K. White, V-Day/4th Universalist Society, Women's Voices, with ***I Am an Emotional Creature*** by Eve Ensler, Central Park West, New York, NY

Non-Kentucky Playwrights with Productions in Kentucky

Blueberry Muffins by Deanna Ableser, 2015 Summer Shorts, Theatre Workshop Owensboro, Owensboro, KY

Out Light by Jane Allard, Shakespeare in Mind, Transylvania University Theatre, Lexington, KY

The Silent Woman by Lydia Blaisdell, produced by Eric Seale, Downtown Arts Center, Lexington, KY

Steel Hammer, **a collaboration** by Anne Bogart/Julia Wolfe/SITI Company: music and lyrics by Julia Wolfe, original text by Kia Corthron, Will Power, Carl Hancock Reux and Regina Taylor with recorded music by the Bang on a Can All-Stars and Trio Medieval, 38th Humana Festival of New American Plays, Actors Theatre of Louisville, Louisville, KY

Winter Games by Rachel Bonds, 38th Humana Festival of New American Plays, Actors Theatre of Louisville, Louisville, KY

He Won't Marry Me by David Carley, 2015 Studio Players 10-Minute Play Festival, Lexington, KY

The Anthropology Section by Patricia Cotter, The Tens: An Evening of 10-minute Plays, Actors Theatre of Louisville, Louisville, KY

I Will Be Gone by Erin Courtney, 39th Humana Festival of New American Plays, Actors Theatre of Louisville, Louisville, KY

Encore, Encore by Colin Speer Crowley, The 17th Year End Series Festival, Northern Kentucky University, Department of Theatre & Dance, Highland Heights, KY

Not Another 9/11 Play by Sonny Das, The Tens: An Evening of 10-minute Plays, Actors Theatre of Louisville, Louisville, KY

Dot by Colman Domingo, 39th Humana Festival of New American Plays, Actors Theatre of Louisville, Louisville, KY

Tomorrow & Tomorrow & Tomorrow & Today by Richard Dresser, Shakespeare in Mind, Transylvania University Theatre, Lexington, KY

and now I only dance at weddings by Jackie Sibblies Drury, Remix 38, 38th Humana Festival of New American Plays, Actors Theatre of Louisville, Louisville, KY

Partners by Dorothy Fortenberry, 38th Humana Festival of New American Plays, Actors Theatre of Louisville, Louisville, KY

is that what I look like? by Idris Goodwin, Remix 38, 38th Humana Festival of New American Plays, Actors Theatre of Louisville, Louisville, KY

The Sharpening Man by Idris Goodwin, Remix 38, 38th Humana Festival of New American Plays, Actors Theatre of Louisville, Louisville, KY

The Grown-Up by Jordon Harrison, 38th Humana Festival of New American Plays, Actors Theatre of Louisville, Louisville, KY

Poor Shem by Gregory Hischak, 38th Humana Festival of New American Plays, Actors Theatre of Louisville, Louisville, KY

The Christians by Lucas Hnath, 38th Humana Festival of New American Plays, Actors Theatre of Louisville, Louisville, KY

Spit, Spat, Spite by Gina Hoben, Shakespeare in Mind, Transylvania University Theatre, Lexington, KY

You Haven't Changed a Bit by Donna Hoke, 2015 Summer Shorts, Theatre Workshop Owensboro, Owensboro, KY

Bath Time is Fun Time by Arthur M. Jolly, Boyle Co. High School, Danville, KY

Long Story by John Kane 2015 Studio Players 10-Minute Play Festival, Lexington, KY

Magic Hour by Jack Karp, 2015 Summer Shorts, Theatre Workshop Owensboro, Owensboro, KY

Last Words by Phillip J. Kaplan, 2015 Summer Shorts, Theatre Workshop Owensboro, Owensboro KY

If. . . Then. . . by Justin Kuritzkes, Remix 38, 38th Humana Festival of New American Plays, Actors Theatre of Louisville, Louisville, KY

brownsville song (b-side for tray) by Kimber Lee, 38th Humana Festival of New American Plays, Actors Theatre of Louisville, Louisville, KY

Canyon's Edge by Barbara Lindsay, 2015 Studio Players 10-Minute Play Festival, Lexington, KY

Canyon's Edge by Barbara Lindsay, 2015 Summer Shorts, Theatre Workshop Owensboro, Owensboro, KY

Scripted by Mark Harvey Levine, 2015 Summer Shorts, Theatre Workshop Owensboro, Owensboro, KY

The Italian Prisoner by Paul Lewis, 2015 Summer Shorts, Theatre Workshop Owensboro, Owensboro, KY

The Markers by Martyna Majok, The Tens: An Evening of 10-minute Plays, Actors Theatre of Louisville, Louisville, KY

A Long Trip by Dan McGeehan, 2015 Summer Shorts, Theatre Workshop Owensboro, Owensboro, KY

New Year's Eve by David MacGregor, 2015 Summer Shorts, Theatre Workshop Owensboro, Owensboro, KY

The Mama and the Papa by Rex McGregor, Smoked Apple Theatre Group, Louisville, KY

Threatened Panda Strikes Back by Rex McGregor, 2015 Studio Players 10-Minute Play Festival, Lexington, KY

Guaranteed by James McLindon, 2015 Studio Players 10-Minute Play Festival, Lexington, KY

The Glory of the World by Charles Mee, 39th Humana Festival of New Plays, Actors Theatre of Louisville, Louisville, KY

The Maltese Walter by John Minigan, 2015 Summer Shorts, Theatre Workshop Owensboro, Owensboro, KY

The Passions of Eugene Gladstone O'Neill by Jo Morello, Downtown Arts Center, Lexington, KY (Balagula Theatre) Winner of the Kentucky Women's Writer's Conference Play Contest

I Was Fine Until You Came In the Room by Rich Orloff, 2015 Summer Shorts, Theatre Workshop Owensboro, Owensboro, KY

Cabin Fever by Brendan Pelsue, The Tens: An Evening of 10-minute Plays, Actors Theatre of Louisville, Louisville, KY

I Promised Myself to Live Faster conceived and created by Pig Iron Theatre Company, Text by Gregory S. Moss and Pig Iron Theatre Company, 39th Humana Festival of New American Plays, Actors Theatre of Louisville, Louisville, KY

Some Prepared Remarks (A History in Speech) by Jason Gray Platt, 38th Humana Festival of New American Plays, Actors Theatre of Louisville, Louisville, KY

a love song//a remix/ by Amelia Roper, Remix 38, 38th Humana Festival of New American Plays, Actors Theatre of Louisville, Louisville, KY

Every Show You've Ever Seen by Amelia Roper, Remix 38, 38th Humana Festival of New American Plays, Actors Theatre of Louisville, Louisville, KY

Bottle of Vodka by Barbara Schendewolf, 2015 Summer Shorts, Theatre Workshop Owensboro, Owensboro, KY

The Blissful Orphans by Kyle John Schmidt, The Tens: An Evening of 10-minute Plays, Actors Theatre of Louisville, Louisville, KY

The Wager by William Sikorsky, 2015 Studio Players 10-Minute Play Festival, Lexington, KY

The Roommate by Jen Silverman, 39th Humana Festival of New American Plays, Actors Theatre of Louisville, Louisville, KY

Iago on the Bus by Dean Staley, Shakespeare in Mind, Transylvania University Theatre, Lexington, KY

It's a Grand Night for Murder by Joe Starczyk, The 17th Year End Series Festival, Northern Kentucky University, Department of Theatre & Dance, Highland Heights, KY

Chicken & Egg Soup by Bob Stewart, 2015 Summer Shorts, Theatre Workshop Owensboro, Owensboro, KY

Kitchen Conversations by Kris Thompson, Summer Shorts, Theatre Workshop Owensboro, Owensboro, KY

Library by Gary Wadley, 2015 Summer Shorts, Theatre Workshop Owensboro, Owensboro, KY

Anniversary by Sam Wallin, 2015 Summer Shorts, Theatre Workshop Owensboro, Owensboro, KY

The Divine Visitor by David L. Williams, The 17th Year End Series Festival, Northern Kentucky University, Department of Theatre & Dance, Highland Heights, KY

So Unnatural a Level by Gary Winter, The Tens: An Evening of 10-minute Plays, Actors Theatre of Louisville, Louisville, KY

Shakespeare's Brainscan by Elizabeth Wong, Shakespeare in Mind, Transylvania University Theatre, Lexington, KY

Reservations Cancelled by John Zygmunt, 2015 Summer Shorts, Theatre Workshop Owensboro, Owensboro, KY

SCREENWRITING SEMINAR
with
Charles Edward Pogue

Hosted by the Kentucky Playwrights Workshop

Though he is a member of the Dramatists Guild of America and Actors Equity, Charles Edward Pogue is probably best known as the screenwriter for such cult films as The Fly and Dragonheart. A graduate of the University of Kentucky with a BA in Theatre, Mr. Pogue moved back to Georgetown several years ago to focus on writing for the stage. For a day we've managed to get him to talk about how to write for film. Learn from the master!

- Venue: The Carnegie Center for Literature and Learning
- Meets: Friday, June 24, 2016
- Time: 1:30 pm - 4:30 pm
- Address:
  251 W. Second Street
  Lexington, KY 40507
  United States
- Cost: $55

Kentucky Playwrights with Readings in Kentucky

With No Where to Go by Shan R. Ayers, Bard's Town Theatre, Louisville, KY

Roscoe-N-Junebug by Stephen R. Bond, Kentucky Theatre Association Conference, Eastern Kentucky University, Richmond, KY, 10-Minute Roots of the Bluegrass New Play Festival, 2015

Madame Buttermilk: A Musical Comedy by Ross Carter, Bluegrass Playwrights Showcase, Studio Players, Lexington, KY

The Two Villages by Richard Cavendish, commissioned by Kentucky Playwrights Workshop, Bo List, Dramaturg, Downtown Arts Center, Lexington, KY

Madder Lake by Tad Chitwood, Derby City Playwrights, Alley Theatre, Louisville, KY

Stages of Bloom: A Midwestern Comedy by Liz Fentress, Bluegrass Playwrights Showcase, Studio Players, Lexington, KY

The Off Chance by Teri Foltz, Pint Sized Plays, The Village Players, Ft. Thomas, KY

Sahara by Teri Foltz, Pint Sized Plays, The Village Players, Ft. Thomas, KY

Dividing Adam's Ashes by A. K. Forbes, Pint Sized Plays, The Village Players, Ft. Thomas, KY

Flight Path by A. K. Forbes, Pint Sized Plays, The Village Players, Ft. Thomas, KY

Lightening Up by Nancy Gall-Clayton, Derby City Playwrights, The Bard's Town Theatre, Louisville, KY

Shakespeare & Thee by Nancy Gall-Clayton, Shape & Flow Writing Instruction, Mellwood Art & Entertainment Center, Louisville, KY

Tex's Great Uncle Ernest by Nancy Gall-Clayton, Shape and Flow Writing Instruction, Louisville, KY

Hair Today by Nancy Gall-Clayton, Kentucky Women's Book Festival, University of Louisville, Chao Auditorium, Louisville, KY

The Fish in the Dumpster by Nancy Gall-Clayton, Kentucky Women's Book Festival, University of Louisville, Chao Auditorium, Louisville, KY

The Fish in the Dumpster by Nancy Gall-Clayton, Vault 1031, Louisville, KY

The Landscape of Tomorrow by Nancy Gall-Clayton, Kentucky Playwrights Workshop, Bo List, Dramaturg, Downtown Arts Center, Lexington, KY

Another Man's Treasure by Ben Gierhart, The Derby City Playwrights, The Bard's Town, Louisville, KY

Stone by Benjamin Graber, Spalding University, Louisville, KY

Riot by Amanda Haan, The Derby City Playwrights, Alley Theatre, Louisville, KY

Buckeye by Elizabeth Harris, Spalding University, Louisville, KY

Nobody Bunny and the Golden Age of Animation by Eli Keel, The Derby City Playwrights, The Vault 1031, Louisville, KY

Sorrow's End by Nathaniel Lachenmeyer, 3 Mondays in July Reading Series, New Works, Inc., Farish Theatre, Lexington Public Library (Downtown), Lexington, KY

Anonymous by Becky LeCron, The Derby City Playwrights, The Vault 1031, Louisville, KY

Widdershins by Kris Lee, Spalding University, Louisville, KY

Something Must be Done by George McGee, commissioned by Kentucky Playwrights Workshop, Bo List, Dramaturg, Downtown Arts Center, Lexington, KY

Vasa Lisa by Kira Obolensky, Spalding University, Louisville, KY

Strangers in the Park by Morgan Patton, Kentucky Theatre Association Conference, Eastern Kentucky University, Richmond KY, Roots of the Bluegrass 10-Minute Play Festival, 2014

The Pretenders by Henrik Ibsen, translation by Charles Edward Pogue, Bluegrass Playwrights Showcase, Studio Players, Lexington, KY

The Goldstein Variations (a musical) by Charlie Schulman and Michael Roberts, Celebration of Recently Published Books by Faculty, Spalding University, Louisville, KY

But is it Art by Dudley Stone, 3 Mondays in July Reading Series, New Works, Inc., Farish Theatre, Lexington Public Library (Downtown), Lexington, KY

The Fly Who Loved Me by Dudley Stone & Christopher Soucy, 3 Mondays in July Reading Series, New Works, Inc., Farish Theatre, Lexington Public Library (Downtown), Lexington, KY

OkayBetterBest by Michael Weems, 3 Mondays in July Reading Series, New Works, Inc., Farish Theatre, Lexington Public Library (Downtown), Lexington, KY

Tender by Bryce Woodard, The Derby City Playwrights, The Bard's Town, Louisville, KY

Balcony: A Verticle Play by Samantha Vakiener, Spalding University, Louisville, KY

Kentucky Playwrights with Readings Outside Kentucky

International

Denmark

Dinner in Minsk by Nancy Gall-Clayton, Belarusian Dream Theatre, Out of Balanz, Copenhagen, Denmark

United Kingdom

Parhelia by Arlene Hutton, Orange Tree Theatre, Richmond, London, UK

United States

The Intervention by Trish Ayers, SHH: Nine 10-Minute Plays with Secrets to be Revealed, the Kentucky Women Playwrights Seminar, Berea, KY, read as part of the Friday Night Footlights Series, Dramatists Guild of America, New York, NY

Keeping Traditions by Sarah Diamond Burroway, ARTS Resources for the Tri-State, Huntington, WV

Botherum by Richard Cavendish, ARTS Resources for the Tri-State, Huntington, WV

Night Music of the River by Richard Cavendish, ARTS Resources for the Tri-State, Huntington, WV

Trouble the Water, But Gently by Karen Devere, SHH: A Collaborative Play, the Kentucky Women Playwrights Seminar, Berea, KY, read as part of the Friday Night Footlights Series, Dramatists Guild of America, New York, NY

Dinner in Minsk by Nancy Gall-Clayton, part of Belarusian Dream Theatre, Majestic Players, Palm Springs, FL

Dinner in Minsk by Nancy Gall-Clayton, part of Belarusian Dream Theatre, Southern Illinois University, Carbondale, IL

In the Pumpkin Patch by Nancy Gall-Clayton, 3Voices (3V) Theatre, New York, NY

Love in the Time of Cockleburs by Nancy Gall-Clayton, ARTS Resources for the Tri-State, Huntington, WV

Pig-A-Boo Appetizers by Nancy Gall-Clayton, Clintonville Community Market, Columbus, OH

Requiem for a Pair of Manicure Scissors: A Monologue by Nancy Gall-Clayton, Here, There & Everywhere, 2014 celebration of International Women's Day, Key City Public Theatre, Port Townsend, WA

Shakespeare & Thee by Nancy Gall-Clayton, Southeastern Theatre Conference Convention, Chattanooga, TN

Wallaroo the Goldfish by Nancy Gall-Clayton, 3Voices (3V) Theatre, New York, NY

End Game by Lacey Gresham, SHH: Nine 10-Minute Plays with Secrets to be Revealed, the Kentucky Women Playwrights Seminar, Berea, KY, read as part of the Friday Night Footlights Series, Dramatists Guild of America, New York, NY

Heirloom by Kristin Hornsby, SHH: Nine 10-Minute Plays with Secrets to be Revealed, the Kentucky Women Playwrights Seminar, Berea, KY, read as part of the Friday Night Footlights Series, Dramatists Guild of America, New York, NY

Eeyore and the Red Warts by Arlene Hutton, Ensemble Studio Theatre, New York, NY

Gated by Arlene Hutton, The Barrow Group, New York, NY

Maria Sibylla by Arlene Hutton, Ensemble Studio Theatre, New York, NY

Maria Sibylla by Arlene Hutton, SPACE on Ryder Farm, Brewster, NY

Safe by Arlene Hutton, Ensemble Studio Theatre, New York, NY

Pilfering Rome by Jonathan Joy, ARTS Resources for the Tri-State, Huntington, WV

Pieces of String by Betty Peterson, SHH: Nine 10-Minute Plays with Secrets to be Revealed, the Kentucky Women Playwrights Seminar, Berea, KY, read as part of the Friday Night Footlights Series, Dramatists Guild of America, New York, NY

Unbeautiful by Donna Phillips, SHH: Nine 10-Minute Plays with Secrets to be Revealed, the Kentucky Women Playwrights Seminar, Berea, KY, read as part of the Friday Night Footlights Series, Dramatists Guild of America, New York, NY

Sheltered Secrets by Patricia Watkins, SHH: Nine 10-Minute Plays with Secrets to be Revealed, the Kentucky Women Playwrights Seminar, Berea, KY, read as part of the Friday Night Footlights Series, Dramatists Guild of America, New York, NY

Zigzag by Brenda White, SHH: Nine 10-Minute Plays with Secrets to be Revealed, the Kentucky Women Playwrights Seminar, Berea, KY, read as part of the Friday Night Footlights Series, Dramatists Guild of America, New York, NY

The Widow's Might by Glenda Dent White, SHH: Nine 10-Minute Plays with Secrets to be Revealed, the Kentucky Women Playwrights Seminar, Berea, KY, read as part of the Friday Night Footlights Series, Dramatists Guild of America, New York, NY

Awards

Roscoe-N-Junebug by Stephen R. Bond, Winner, Kentucky Theatre Association, Lexington, KY, 10-Minute Roots of the Bluegrass New Play Contest, 2015

It's Just a Box by Sarah Diamond Burroway, People's Choice Best Play, 2015 New Play Festival, J.B. Sowards Theatre, Ashland Community & Technical College, Ashland, KY

Strange Things Happen by Chelsea Fannin, People's Choice Best Play, 2014 New Play Festival, J.B. Sowards Theatre, Ashland Community & Technical College, Ashland, KY

Lightening Up by Nancy Gall-Clayton, Runner-up for the Robert Pickering Award, Coldwater Community Theatre, Coldwater, MI

Boxes by Catherine Goguen & J. Michael Radford, Finalist, Kentucky Theatre Association, Lexington, KY, Roots of the Bluegrass New Play Contest, 2015

A Passing Moment by John J. Kelly, Finalist, Kentucky Theatre Association, Lexington, KY, Roots of the Bluegrass New Play Contest, 2014

Art Meets Activism, grant to Basil Kreimendahl from the Kentucky Foundation for Women, for theatre work with the transgender community in Louisville

The Passions of Eugene Gladstone O'Neill by Jo Morello
Downtown Arts Center, Lexington, KY (Balagula Theatre), Winner of the Kentucky Women's Writer's Conference Play Contest

Aiden's Gift by Elizabeth Shear Orendorff, First Prize, Silverthorne Theatre Company, Greenfield, MA

Philip Paradis selected Playwright-in-Residence, Manhattan Repertory Theater, New York, NY
Strangers in the Park by Morgan Patton, Winner, Kentucky Theatre Association, Lexington, KY, Roots of the Bluegrass 10-Minute Play Contest
According to John by David John Preece, Finalist, Kentucky Theatre Association, Lexington, KY, Roots of the Bluegrass New Play Contest, 2014
Drinking Perfume by Lindsay Price, Winner of the Bard Award, The Bard's Town Theatre, Louisville, KY

Poor Little Edward by Cody Taylor, Finalist, Kentucky Theatre Association, Lexington, KY, Roots of the Bluegrass New Play Contest, 2015

CPR on the Lost Continent by Brian Walker, Winner, Kentucky Theatre Association, Lexington, KY, Roots of the Bluegrass New Play Contest, 2015
Gamers 4 Life by Brian Walker was a finalist for the Heideman award, Actors Theatre of Louisville, Louisville, KY

SNAPDRAGON:
A Journal of Creativity

Snapdragon accepts submissions of previously produced 10-minute plays for publication in literary format from resident Kentucky playwrights ONLY. Playwrights retain all rights to their plays. Snapdragon will **not** act as an agent for the plays it publishes; inquiries regarding possible production of the published works will be forwarded to the playwright. Plays published elsewhere will not be considered. Two or more plays published annually. Payment is one contributor copy.

Snapdragon gives preference to writers living outside Kentucky in considering submissions of:
- Poetry to fifteen lines per poem, submit a maximum of three (3) poems
- Short essays to 2,500 words
- Short stories to 2,500 words
- Novel excerpts to 5,000 words
- Art, black and white only
- Photographs, 300 dpi or higher, .jpg
  (color for cover consideration, b/w for interior)

Payment for submissions is one contributor copy.

Submissions to: Jeanine Grant Lister, editor
Snapdragon
JW Books
PO Box 143
Cynthiana, KY 41010
or by email to: jeaninegrantlister@gmail.com

Part Two:

Kentucky Theatres that Produced New Plays

Editor's Note: Following is a list of the theatres—high school, college, community, summer, and professional—that presented productions of new plays during the calendar years 2014 and 2015. Though some theatres also did readings, those are not listed here. Instead, the readings can be found in the playwright listings. To the extent possible, contact information for each theatre is also listed. The exception to this is information about high schools, for which information is not included at all. Plays produced are listed alphabetically by last name of the first playwright listed.

Kentucky

Actors & Playwrights Collaborative, with New Edgecliff Theatre
Phil Paradis, Director
http://soldierschristmas.net/actorsandplaywrights
(859)653-6344
Soldier's Christmas by Philip Paradis

Actors Theatre of Louisville
316 West Main St.
Louisville, KY 40202
Les Waters, Artistic Director
Jennifer Bielstein, Managing Director
http://actorstheatre.org
The Rear View Mirror by Kristin Bell

Actors Theatre of Louisville, Cont.

Steel Hammer, a collaboration by Anne Bogart/Julia Wolfe/SITI Company: music and lyrics by Julia Wolfe, original text by Kia Corthron, Will Power, Carl Hancock Reux and Regina Taylor with recorded music by the Bang on a Can All-Stars and Trio Medieval.
6,600 Volts by Robin Carroll
The Torpedo Room by Benjamin Collins
I Will be Gone by Erin Courtney
The Anthropology Section by Patricia Cotter
Not Another 9/11 Play by Sonny Das
Dot by Colman Domingo
and now I only dance at weddings by Jackie Sibblies Drury
is that what I look like by Idris Goodwin
The Sharpening Man by Idris Goodwin
A Haunting in the East Wing by Katie Henning
Finger Play (not a real title) by Basil Kreimendahl
Like We Do by Basil Kreimendahl
If...Then... by Justin Kuritzkes
War of Attrition by Justin Kuritzkes
The Markers by Martyna Majok
The Glory of the World by Charles Mee
A Starfish's World by Brooke Morrison
The Wedding Guest by Steve Moulds
Cabin Fever by Brendan Pelsue
I Promised Myself to Live Faster, conceived and created by Pig Iron Theatre Company, Text by Gregory S Moss and Pig Iron Theatre Company
The Q & A by John Rooney
A love song//a remix/ by Amelia Roper
The Flingin' Wisbees by Kallen Sebastian

Actors Theatre of Louisville, Cont.
The Blissful Orphans by Kyle John Schmidt
The Roommate by Jen Silverman
Don't Leave Me Here, Okay? By Annie Stone
Street Smarts by Lauren Titus
Sick by Huy Vo
So Unnatural a Level by Gary Winter

Artist Asylum Theatre
Elizabethtown, KY
Reindeer by Richard Cavendish
The Two Villages by Richard Cavendish
A Curiosity Quilt by Nancy Gall-Clayton
The Landscape of Tomorrow by Nancy Gall-Clayton
My Father Thinks He's Irish by George McGee.
Something Must be Done by George McGee
Sunny Side by Philip Paradis
Visitation Privileges by Brian Walker

Ashland Community & Technical College
1400 College Drive
Ashland, KY
Jon Joy, Theatre Program Director
Until Death by Malynda Brooke Barker
Little Girl Lost by Malynda Brook Barker
It's Just a Box by Sarah Diamond Burroway
To the Woman at Food Fair Who Screamed at Her Child
    by Sarah Diamond Burroway
Earl by Charles "Chase" Davaney
Strange Things Happen by Chelsea G. Fannin
I Hate Vampires by Jessica K. Howard
Polynomial Dysfunction by Jessica K. Howard
Building Bridges by Mary Shortridge

Ashland Community & Technical College, Cont.
Retribution by Mary Shortridge
The Gifted Tree by Mary Shortridge

Baby Horse Theatre Group
Louisville, KY
Facebook: facebook.com/babyhorsetheatre
Jon Becraft and Kelli Fitzgibbons, founders
Louisville Championship Arm Wrestling: WRIST IN PEACE (sic) devised by Baby Horse Theatre Group

Bard's Town Theatre
1801 Bardstown Road, Louisville, KY
Doug Schutte, Artistic Director
http://www.thebardstowntheatre.org
(502)749-5275
Oedipus Rex: The Original MF created by The Bard's Town Theatre Company
It's Just a Box by Sarah Diamond Burroway
A Deal by Nancy Gall-Clayton
A Trip to Eden by Nancy Gall-Clayton
The Landscape of Tomorrow by Nancy Gall-Clayton
Levels of Living by Nancy Gall-Clayton
Zimy & Zog Visit Earth by Nancy Gall-Clayton
Chasing Ophelia, by Doug Schutte
The Kings of Christmas by Doug Schutte
Hero Worship by Brian Walker

Baron's Theatre
131 Main Street
Louisville, KY 40202
Joanne Caridis
Email: whiskeyrowlofts@essentialdetails.biz
(502)499-6478
Dante's Memory Tomb by Rachel White

Berea Arena Theatre
Location:
1835 Big Hill Road
Berea, KY
Mailing Address:
Berea Arena Theatre
1 Fairway Drive
Berea, KY 40403
Email: bereaarenatheater@gmail.com
(859)986-9039
The Intervention by Trish Ayers
Trouble the Water, But Gently by Karen Devere
End Game by Lacey Gresham
Heirloom by Kristin Hornsby
Pieces of String by Betty Peterson
Unbeautiful by Donna Phillips
Sheltered Secrets by Patricia Watkins
Zigzag by Brenda White
The Widow's Might by Glenda Dent White

Berea College Theatre
Jelkyl Building, CPO 1947
Berea, KY
Deborah Martin, Chair
https://www.berea.edu/thr/
(859)985-3300
Carry On by Trish Ayers
The Poet from Pikeville by Nancy Gall-Clayton
Remedial Lessons by Arlene Hutton
Southern Beauty by Brenda K. White

Bunbury Theatre
Henry Clay Building, 3rd Floor
604 South Third Street
Louisville, KY 40202
Juergen K. Tossman, Artistic Director
Email: bunburytheatre@gmail.com
http://www.bunburytheatre.org
A Homeless Holiday by Juergen K. Tossman
Bonhoffer the Last Encounter by Juergen K. Tossman
Forgive Me it's Christmas by Juergen K. Tossman
Eeenie Meany by Teresa Willis

Cisco Montgomery, Inc.
P.O. Box 3264,
Louisville, KY 40208.
Contact: Lawrence Muhammed
Murder the Devil by Cisco Montgomery
Radio Play by Cisco Montgomery
Kin Under the Skin by Cisco Montgomery
Boomerang by Cisco Montgomery

Eve Theatre Company
Louisville, KY
Diane Stretz-Thurmond, Susan Lynch, Charlotte Hammett Hubrich, and Kim Butterweck, co-founders
Email: evetheatrelouisville@gmail.com
http://www.evetheatrecopmany.com
(502)759-1912
You Better Sit Down: Tales from My Parents' Divorce,
 written or created by Anne Kaufman, Mathew Maher, Caitlin Miller, Jennifer R. Morris, Janice Paran, and Robbie Collier Sublet

Frog Pump Productions
Fisherville, KY
Sex Again by Heidi Saunders Walker

Jenny Wiley Theatre
218 Second Street,
Pikeville, KY 41501
AND
121 Theatre Court,
Prestonsburg, KY 41653
http://www.jwtheatre.com/
(877) 225-5598 x217
The Big Sandy River Plays (Feud; Firebrand; Fresh Water) by Michael Ross Albert

Kentucky Black Repertory Theatre
Louisville, KY
Contact through Cisco Montgomery, Inc.
Buster! The Musical by Larry Muhammad

Kentucky Playwrights Workshop, Inc.
PO Box 59
Corinth, KY 41010
Bill McCann, Jr., president
All shows performed at the Kentucky State Fair, Louisville, KY
Rose Upon a White Gait by Tammy Brady
Wash Day by Sarah Diamond Burroway
Reindeer by Richard Cavendish
Flight Path by A.K. Forbes
Zombie Love by Jennifer Johnson
Namaste by Stephanie Porter

Kentucky Shakespeare Festival
323 W. Broadway Suite 401
Louisville, KY 40202
Matt Wallace, Producing Artistic Director
Email: info@kyshakespeare.com
http://www.kyshakespeare.com
(502)574-9900 main
The Two Lobbyists of Verona by Diana Grisanti and Steve Moulds
Chasing Ophelia by Doug Schutte

Kincaid Regional Theatre
500 South Chapel Street
Falmouth, KY
http://www.krtshow.com/
Where Are You Christmas? by John Seidenberg II

Knox Central High School
Barbourville, KY
Looking for Mr. Right by Catherine Rhoden Goguen

Looking For Lilith Theatre Company
312 Crescent Ct.
Louisville, KY 40206
Email: info@lookingforlilith.org
(502)638-2559
Sidewinders by Basil Kreimendahl
Prevailing Winds by Looking For Lilith Theatre

Louisville Improvisors, Inc.
Email: louisvilleimprovisors@gmail.com
(702)672-9121
The Buddy Glim Show, created/improvised by the ensemble

Louisville Repertory Theatre
2822 Goose Creek Road
Louisville, KY 40242-2202
Email: LRCTheatre@outlook.com
http://www.lourep.com/
dirty sexy derby play by Brian Walker

Lindsey Wilson College
Department of Theatre
V.P. Henry Auditorium
210 Lyndsey Wilson Street
Columbia, KY
Robert Brock, Assistant Professor of Theatre
Email: brockr@lindsey.edu
(270)590-4803
Angels My Father Sent by Erika Finley

Marrow Street Theatre
Louisville, KY
Tad Chitwood, Brian Hinds, and Rachel White, founders
Blizzard of '92 by Rachel White

Northern Kentucky University
Corbett Theatre
NKU Fine Arts Center
FA 259; Nunn Drive
Highland Heights, KY 41099
(859)572-5464
Soldier's Christmas by Philip Paradis

Northern Kentucky University
School of the Arts
Department of Theatre and Dance
Highland Heights, KY
Michael Hatton, Department Chair
The Road through Damascus by Robert Macke
The Trouble with Boys by Alexx Rouse
The River Shore by Abigail Walker,
The Sundial Enthusiast by Abigail Walker,

Pioneer Playhouse
840 Stanford Road
Danville, Kentucky 40422
Charlotte Henson, Producer
Robby Henson, Artistic Director
Heather Henson, Managing Director
Email: pioneerplayhouse@att.net
(866)KYplays ((866)597-5297)
Local: (859)236-2747
Walking Across Egypt by Catherine Bush (adapted from the novel by Clyde Edgerton)

Pioneer Playhouse, Cont.
The Wonder Team by Robby Henson
Grounded, adapted by Chelsea Marcantel
Who Dunnit, Darling? by Charles Edward Pogue and
    Larry Drake

The Public Theatre of Kentucky
545 Morris Alley
Bowling Green, KY 42101
Amber Turner, Producing Director
www.ptkbg.org
(270)781-6233
Sleepy Hollow by Harper Lee

Roh's Theatre Company
Roh's Opera House
133 E. Pike Street
Cynthiana, KY 41031
Mike Bess, President
http://rohstheatrecompany.com
(859)234-9803
Little Red by Gil Rognstad

Rose Barn Theatre
P.O. Box 66
Richmond, KY 40475
http://rosebarntheatre.com/
(859)893-7778
Stan O'Donald's Retro Radio Review by Rose Barn cast
    and director
But is it Art? by Dudley Stone

Savage Rose Classical Theatre Company
PO Box 17012
Louisville, KY 40217
Kelly Moore, Artistic Director
Email: kelly.moore.savagerose@gmail.com
(502)930-4697
The Maids by Jean Genet, adapted by Tad Chitwood

Studio Players
154 W. Bell Court
Lexington, KY
Bob Singleton, President
http://studioplayers.org
He Won't Marry Me by David Carley
What Would Jesus Pack? by Ross Carter
Long Story by John Kane
Canyon's Edge by Barbara Lindsay
Threatened Panda Strikes Back by Rex McGregor
Guaranteed by James McLindon
The Wager by William Sikorsky

Theatre [502]
PO Box 4875
Louisville, KY 40204
Contact: Amy Attaway
http://www.theatre502.org
Bull by Mike Bartlett
The Two Lobbyists of Verona by Diana Grisanti and Steve
    Moulds
The Stanger and Ludlow Quinn by Steve Moulds and
    Diana Grisanti
Ocar's Successor(s) by Brian Walker

Theatre Farouche
465 Rose Street
FA 114
Lexington, KY 40506
Nancy C. Jones, Artistic Director
The Lesson by Eugene Ionesco, translated by Nancy C. Jones

Theatre Workshop Owensboro
407 W. 5th Street
Owensboro, KY 42301
Executive Director: Todd Reynolds
Production Manager: Damon Wallace
http://www.theatreworkshop.org/
(270)683-5333
Blueberry Muffins by Deanna Ableser
You Haven't Changed a Bit by Donna Hoke
Last Words by Phillip J. Kaplan
Magic Hour by Jack Karp
Among the Quick and the Dead by John Kelly
Scripted by Mark Harvey Levine
Theater Workshop Owensboro, Cont.
The Italian Prisoner by Paul Lewis
Canyon's Edge by Barbara Lindsay
New Year's Eve by David McGregor
A Long Trip by Dan McGeehan
I Was Fine Until You Came Into the Room by Rich Orloff
Chicken & Egg Soup by Bob Stewart
Kitchen Conversations by Kris Thompson
Anniversary by Sam Wallin
Library by Gary Wadley
Trigger Happy by Rebecca Wright
Reservations Cancelled by John Zymunt

Think Tank Theatre
Louisville, KY
Tony Dingman and Kyle Ware, founders
Facebook: facebook.com/ThinkTankTheatreLouisville
Ton of Bricks, created and performed by the ensemble

University of the Cumberlands
Kohn Theatre
6178 College Station Dr.
Williamsburg, KY 40769
Dr. Kimberly Miller, Artistic Director
Email: kim.miller@ucumberlands.edu
The Choice by Jillian Carpenter

The Village Players
8 N. Ft. Thomas Avenue
Ft. Thomas, KY, 41075
Email: info@the-village-players.com
http://the-village-players.com
The Great Debate by Philip Paradis
The Kitty Cat Ultimatum by Philip Paradis

Walden Theatre/Blue Apple Players
1123 Payne Street
Louisville, KY 40204
Artistic Director – Charlie Sexton
Managing Director – Alison Huff
Email: mail@waldentheatre.org
http://www.waldentheatre.org
(502)589-0084
Glass Carousel by Jacob Craigo-Snell

Walden Theatre/Blue Apple Players, Cont.
Days Gone By by Will Devary
Want You Back by Kora Duvall
#NotAllMen by Ruthie Dworkin
Looks Can Be Deceiving by Delaney Hildreth
Anita Maan by Ruby Osborne
Jane the Plain by August Schulenburg
The Snow Queeen (sic) by Stanton Wood, based on the Hans Christian Anderson story

Western Kentucky University
Department of Theatre and Dance
1906 College Heights Blvd. #71086
Bowling Green, KY 42101-1086
David Young, Department Chair
Email: theatredanceoffice@wku.edu
http://www.wku.edu/theatre-and-dance
(270)745-5845
Inedicabilis, created by Keifer Adkins and Sam O'Mara
Armistice by Isaac Barnes
Luna by Lena Buechler
Marilyn by Isiah Fish
Stay, written and performed by Isiah Fish
An Expressive Existence, created by Eric Mattingly and the Ensemble
You Hear Me Speak by Dare Norman
Kentucky October by Sam O'Mara
Purgatwar by Miranda Swan
Puzzle Piece by Elliott Talkington
Patchworked, written and performed by Becca Trimbur

Woodford Theatre
Falling Springs Arts & Recreation Center
Beasley Road
Versailles, KY 40483
A Kentucky Christmas adapted by James W. Rodgers

New Plays Produced at Non-Traditional Venues in Kentucky

Editor's Note: Addresses and contact information for these producers are not listed because they do not regularly produce theatrical productions and are probably not well equipped to field enquiries regarding future productions. Also included are venues and entities in which more than one theatre and more than one producer was involved.

Breeder's Cup Festival
Lexington, KY
I Dedicate this Ride—The Life And Times of Isaac Murphy by Frank X. Walker

The Capital City Museum
Frankfort, KY
Two Loves and a River by Don Coffey

The Filson Historical Society
Louisville, KY
Double V by Larry Muhammad

Keeneland Library
Lexington, KY
This Was Racing: An Evening with Joe Palmer by Walter May

Kentucky State Fair
The Kentucky New Play Series
Kentucky Playwrights Workshop, Inc.
PO Box 59
Corinth, KY 41010
Bill McCann, Producer
Cheryl Lyn Brumley, Associate Producer
Rose Upon a White Gait by Tammy Brady
Wash Day by Sarah Diamond Burroway
Reindeer by Richard Cavendish
Flight Path by A.K. Forbes
A Curiosity Quilt by Nancy Gall-Clayton
Zombie Love by Jennifer Johnson
My Father Thinks He's Irish by George McGee
Sunny Side by Philip Paradis
Namaste by Stephanie Porter
When Grandma Davis Hit the Glass by Rebecca Ryland
Visitation Privileges by Brian Walker

Kentucky Women's Book Festival
University of Louisville
Chao Auditorium
Louisville, KY
Hair Today by Nancy Gall-Clayton
The Fish in the Dumpster by Nancy Gall-Clayton

New Plays by Kentucky Playwrights Performed at Theatres or Venues Outside Kentucky

International

Canada

George McDougal High School
Airdrie, AB, Canada
May I Have Your Attention, Please? By Catherine Rhoden Goguen

La Crete Public School
La Crete, AB, Canada
May I Have Your Attention, Please? By Catherine Rhoden Goguen

Hespeler Library
Cambridge ON, Canada
The Anesthetic was Psalms by Nancy Gall-Clayton

Scotland

Edinburgh Fringe Festival
180 High Street
Edinburgh EH1 1QS Scotland
United Kingdom
Telephone: +44 (0)131 226 0026
Email: admin@edfringe.com
Kissed the Girls and Made Them Cry by Arlene Hutton

United States

Arizona

Sun City Players Community Theatre
Sun City, AZ
Greg Engstrom, President
Website: http://www.suncityplayerscommunitytheater.org
Liz's Circus Story by Liz Fentress

California

The Charles Stewart Howard Playhouse
Mailing Address:
22518 Burbank Blvd.
Woodland Hills, CA 91367
Theatre Address:
21338 Dumetz Ave.
Woodland Hills, CA 91367
Marshelle Giggles-Mills, Artistic Director
Email: whctheatre@gmail.com
Keeping Traditions by Sarah Diamond Burroway

Lucky Penny Productions
Location:
Community Arts Center
1758 Industrial Way, Suite 208
Napa, CA
Mail: Lucky Penny Productions
1357 Foster Road
Napa CA 94558
Taylor Bartolucci, Co-Founder and Artistic/Casting
    Director

Lucky Penny Productions, Cont.
Barry Martin, Co-Founder and Managing Director
Email: info@luckypennynapa.com
(707)266-6305
Interrogation by James Colgan

The Mirror Theatre
4934 Lankershim Blvd
North Hollywood, California
http://www.mirrortheater.com/
(818)732-1192
Sunny Side Up by Philip Paradis

North Park Vaudeville & Candy Shoppe
North Park Playwright Festival
2031 El Cajon Blvd.
San Diego, CA 92104
http://northparkvaudeville.com/
(619)220-8663
Painting the Egress by Trish Ayers
Straight Out of the Closet Trish Ayers
Magpie by Teri Foltz
Have a Nice Day by Elizabeth Shear Orendorff
The Great Debate by Philip Paradis

West Chester Enriched Sciences Magnets (high school)
Los Angeles, CA 90045-2322
May I Have Your Attention, Please? by Catherine Rhoden
    Goguen

Connecticut

Playhouse on Park
244 Park Road
West Hartford, CT 06119
Tracy Flater, co-founder, Executive Director
Sean Harris, co-founder, Artistic Director
Darlene Zoller, co-founder, Artistic Director
Sasha Bratt, Literary Manager
Submissions: newworks@PlayhouseTheatreGroup.org
http://playhouseonpark.org
(860)523-5900
Kissed the Girls and Made Them Cry by Arlene Hutton

Delaware

The Arden Club
(The Arden Club Theatre)
2126 The Highway, Arden,
Wilmington, DE 19810
http://ardenclub.org/
(302)475-3126
May I Have Your Attention, Please? by Catherine Rhoden Goguen

Kansas

Osawatomie High School
Osawatomie, KS
Looking for Mr. Right by Catherine Rhoden Goguen

Maryland

Great Mills High School
Great Mills, MD
Looking for Mr. Right by Catherine Rhoden Goguen

Massachusetts

Silverthorne Theatre Company
PO Box 204
Turners Falls, MA 01376
(413)768-7514
Aiden's Gift by Elizabeth Shear Orendorff

Minnesota

Pillsbury Baptist College
315 S Grove
Owatonna, MN 55060
www.pillsbury.edu
(507)451-2710
May I Have Your Attention, Please? by Catherine Rhoden Goguen

Nevada

Palo Verde High School
Las Vegas, NV
Looking for Mr. Right by Catherine Rhoden Goguen

New York

Alice Griffin Jewel Box Theatre
The Pershing Square Signature Center
480 West 42nd Street
New York, NY 10036
Night is a Room by Naomi Wallace

The Barrow Group
312 West 36th Street, 3rd Floor
New York, NY 10013
Seth Barrish and Lee Brock, co-Artistic Directors
Robert Serrell, Executive Director
https://www.barrowgroup.org
(212)760-2615
Kissed the Girls and Made Them Cry by Arlene Hutton

Brooklyn College
Department of Theatre
2800 Bedford Avenue
Brooklyn, NY 11210
Victor (Kip) Marsh, Associate Professor, Theatre
    Department Chairperson
Double Entendre by Nancy Gall-Clayton

Gerald Schoenfeld Theatre
236 W 45th St New York, NY 10036
http://www.shubert.nyc/theatres/gerald-schoenfeld/
The Bridges of Madison County, music & lyrics by Jason
    Robert Brown, book by Marsha Norman

La Mama Experimental Theatre
Ellen Stewart Theatre/The Downstairs/
Box Office/Archives & Administrative Office
66 East 4th Street
New York, NY 10003
http://lamama.org
 (646)430-5374
The Maids by Jean Genet, translated by Nancy C. Jones

Manhattan Repertory Theatre
303 West 42nd St. at 8th Ave.
New York, NY
Breaking Gulf News by Phil Paradis
Daddy's Little Girl by Phil Paradis
God Is A Ford Man by Phil Paradis
The Holey Swiss Duet by Phil Paradis
The Powder Puff Heist by Phil Paradis
Sunny Side by Phil Paradis

Signature Theatre Company
The Pershing Square Signature Center
480 West 42nd Street
New York, NY 10036
And I and Silence by Naomi Wallace
The Liquid Plain by Naomi Wallace

3Voices (3V) Theatre
New York, NY
Aliza Shane, Founding Artist/Co-Artistic Director
Jenn Tufaro, Founding Artist/Co-Artistic Director
Chandra Calentine, Founding Artist/Creative Consultant
Email: 3vtheatre@gmail.com
http://www.3vtheatre.com
In the Pumpkin Patch by Nancy Gall-Clayton
Wallaroo the Goldfish by Nancy Gall-Clayton

North Dakota

Dakota Prairie High School
Petersburg, ND
May I Have Your Attention, Please? by Catherine Rhoden
 Goguen

Ohio

Brecksville Theater on the Square
PO Box 41002
Brecksville, Ohio 44141
Diana Strongosky – President
Jackie Royak - Administrator
Email: Theater@BTOTS.org
(440)526-3443
May I Have Your Attention, Please? by Catherine Rhoden
 Goguen

Tri-County Players
Sharonville, OH
www.tricountyplayers.org
Email: info@tricountyplayers.org
The Search for Tinker Doyle by Elizabeth Shear Orendorff

Pennsylvania

Philadelphia Modern Orthodox High School
Philadelphia, PA
Shakespeare and Thee by Nancy Gall-Clayton

South Carolina

Abbeville Opera House
Post Office Box 247
Abbeville, South Carolina, 29620
Executive Director, Michael Genevie
Email: operahouse@wctel.net
http://www.theabbevilleoperahouse.com
Abbeville Opera House, Cont.
(864) 366-2157
May I Have Your Attention, Please? by Catherine Rhoden
 Goguen

South of Broadway Theatre
1080 E Montague Ave,
North Charleston, SC 29405
http://southofbroadway.com
(843)745-0317
Rosencrantz and Guildenstern Are Not Dead by Fredric
 DeJaco

Center Stage
Location: 501 River Street
Address: Post Office Box 8451
Greenville, SC 29604
Executive Artistic Director Glenda ManWaring
Email:information@centrestage.org
(864)233-6733
A Flea in Her Ear, adapted by Charles Edward Pogue

Cambridge Academy
Greenwood, SC
May I Have Your Attention, Please? by Catherine Rhoden Goguen

Texas

Bovina High School
Bovina, Texas
Looking for Mr. Right by Catherine Rhoden Goguen

The Company Onstage Theatre
536 Westbury Square
Houston, TX 77035
Email: info@companyonstage.org
http://www.companyonstage.org/
(713)726-1219
The Palmetto Family, by Nancy Gall-Clayton

Wisconsin

Ripon High School
Ripon, WI
May I Have Your Attention, Please? by Catherine Rhoden
    Goguen

New Plays by Kentucky Playwrights Performed at Non-Traditional Theatres or Venues Outside Kentucky

Editor's Note: Addresses and contact information for these producers are not listed because they do not regularly produce theatrical productions and are not generally equipped to field enquiries regarding future productions.

New York
V-Day/4th Universalist Society, as part of Women's Voices, *I am an Emotional Creature* by Eve Ensler
Central Park West
New York, NY
To the Woman at Food Fair Who Screamed at Her Child by Sarah Diamond Burroway
Southern Beauty by Brenda K. White

Midtown International Theatre Festival
Short Play Lab
New York, NY
http://www.midtownfestival.org/
The Off Chance by Teri Foltz

National Museum of Racing
Saratoga Springs, NY
This Was Racing: An Evening with Joe Palmer by Walter May

Ohio
The 6th Annual Women of Appalachia's Women Speak Event
Arts/West
Athens, Ohio
Dinner Bucket by Sarah Diamond Burroway
Signing Off by Sarah Diamond Burroway

The 6th Annual Women of Appalachia's Women Speak Event
PVG Artisans
Chillicothe, Ohio
Signing Off by Sarah Diamond Burroway

Playwright Support and Training

Editor's Note: The organizations in this section are those which have as their mission helping playwrights develop their skills, or otherwise offer opportunities that will benefit them directly or indirectly. All are non-profits or governmental organizations. Some charge fees, others do not.

Actors & Playwrights Collaborative
Fort Thomas
By invitation only to actors and playwrights living/working in Northern Kentucky. Contact: Phil Paradis phil.paradis@fuse.net

Carnegie Center for Literacy & Learning
251 West Second Street
Lexington, Kentucky 40507
Neil Chethik, Executive Director
Bill McCann, Jr., Playwright Mentor
Email: ccll1@carnegiecenterlex.org
Phone: (859)254-4175 / Fax: (859)281-1151
Offers classes in playwriting and screenwriting, though the general focus is on other literary pursuits such as poetry, fiction, non-fiction, and writing for children.

Derby City Playwrights
Louisville, KY
Brian Walker, Artistic Director
https://www.facebook.com/derbycityplaywrights
Louisville area playwrights meet regularly over a one-year period to write and develop their own new works through meetings, readings and productions. Participants chosen through a submission and selection process.

Kentucky Playwrights Workshop, Inc.
PO Box 59
Corinth, KY 41010
Email: Ky.playwright@yahoo.com
A 501(c)3 non-profit public charity that provides opportunities to Kentucky playwrights to have their work produced at the Kentucky State Fair as part of the Kentucky New Play Series; to meet and network with other playwrights at conferences and other training events; periodically the organization also commissions Kentucky playwrights to write new works for the stage. Follow KPW on Facebook or contact ky.playwright@yahoo.com.

New Play Slam
Vault 1031
1031 South Sixth St
Louisville
Gathering at 6:45; casting followed by reading at 7:00; discussion follows each reading. The meetings are held periodically during the academic year. Meetings held monthly for playwrights and actors. Playwrights can have 10-12 page excerpts from new works read by some of the community's fine actors. Discussions of each play follow the reading. For more information about how to request a time and date to have work read, contact newplayslam@gmail.com. Actors can simply show up.

Kentucky Contests, Festivals, and Opportunities

Humana Festival of New American Plays and other submission opportunities
Actors Theatre of Louisville
316 West Main St.
Louisville, KY 40202
Les Waters, Artistic Director
Jennifer Bielstein, Managing Director
http://actorstheatre.org
Facebook
National 10-Minute Play Contest ATL accepts plays 10 pages/10 minutes in length.
The New Voices Ten-Minute Play Contest accepts plays written by middle and high school students from the Louisville Metro area.
Humana Festival of New American Plays
Information about how to submit for any of these programs can be found at:
http://actorstheatre.org/participate/play-submissions/

Bellarmine University
International 10-minute Play Festival
Megan Burnett, MFA
Theatre Program Director
Assistant Professor of Theatre
Bellarmine University
2001 Newburg Road
Louisville, KY 40205
Email: mburnett@bellarmine.edu
(502)272-7480
A themed 10-minute play contest. Visit the department's website for information: http://www.bellarmine.edu/cas/theatre/season/festival

Kentucky New Play Series
Kentucky Playwrights Workshop, Inc.
PO Box 59
Corinth, KY 41010
Bill McCann, President
A play contest open to resident Kentucky playwrights 16 and older. Plays must be 10-15 minutes in length. Up to six (6) plays are selected to be presented at the Kentucky State Fair. Plays must be comedies appropriate for family members aged 3–93! Winners paid a $25 per performance in lieu of royalties payment. Inquiries to ky.playwright@yahoo.com

Kentucky Voices
Pioneer Playhouse
840 Stanford Road
Danville, KY 40422
Pioneer Playhouse Artistic Director Robby Henson is interested in reading new comedies rooted in Kentucky history for possible inclusion in the theatre's Kentucky Voices series. Send queries, by mail only, to Mr. Henson's attention at the above address. Do not call or email.

Kentucky Women's Writer's Conference Play Contest
University of Kentucky
College of Arts & Sciences
202 Patterson Office Tower
Lexington KY, 40506-0027
(859)257-8354
Bi-monthly listserv of updates about the contest and more: kentuckywomenwriters@gmail.com.
The Kentucky Women Writers Conference awards a biennial Prize for Women Playwrights to bring more scripts by women to the stage, through a collaboration among our program, a partnering theater, and a guest judge. The winner receives a world premiere production for a paying audience, with royalties, plus a cash prize of $500.

Roots of the Bluegrass New Play Contest
Kentucky Theatre Association
c/o Lexington Children's Theatre
418 W. Short Street
Lexington, KY 40507
Adanma Barton, president (859) 985-3258
Steve Cleberg, Contest Coordinator
http://theatreky.org/index.php/programs/playwright-festival
Summary: Two divisions: Full-Length and 10-Minute. Play submissions due during the summer. Finalist and winning playwrights given readings of cuttings from their full-length works; winning 10-minute plays read in their entirety at November KTA Conference. Cash awards for winners of each division. Visit website for more info.

Snapdragon: A Journal of Creativity
JW Books
PO Box 143
Cynthiana, KY 40131
Email: jeaninegrantlister@gmail.com
Jeanine Lister, editor
Snapdragon publishes short stories, essays, short plays, black and white photographs and art twice a year. Submission: ongoing. One to five 10-minute plays are published in each issue. Preference is given to resident Kentucky playwrights when considering 10-minute plays for publication.

Summer Shorts Contest and Festival
Theatre Workshop Owensboro
www.theatreworkshop.org
Follow on Facebook

Summary: Building on the success of 2015's festival, TWO's Summer Shorts returns for another run at the Trinity Center, in downtown Owensboro, KY. This year TWO will select 8-10 plays for production over 2 weekends in June. This year there will also be a small entry fee ($15) for submissions but there are cash prizes ($400 and $200) for the 2 top plays in both categories! Visit the website for more information.

TenTucky 10-Minute Play Contest (and Festival)
Bard's Town Theatre
1801 Bardstown Road, Louisville, KY
Doug Schutte, Artistic Director
http://www.thebardstowntheatre.org/
(502)749-5275

Rules and submission information is available on the theatre's website. Winning plays will be performed as part of the Ten-Tucky Festival, fall 2016

Y.E.S. (Year-End Series) Play Festival
Northern Kentucky University
Sandra Forman, Professor
& Y.E.S. Project Director
(859)572-6303

N.K.U.'s Department of Theatre produced its first Y.E.S. festival in 1983, premiering three new works. Y.E.S. was designed to be a biennial festival occurring in odd numbered years. We produce scripts that cannot have had a previous professional or university production. In some years we have actually produced four shows and several times we have included Staged Readings to complement the Main Stage productions. To date, we have produced over 50 new works, most of which have been published, and several have had Off-Broadway productions. Of the 400-500 scripts that we receive, many are from abroad. This past festival we received submissions from Canada, England, Israel, Portugal, and Siberia as well as every state in the U.S. We are proud of gaining an international following.

We will accept submissions from May 1 through September 30, 2016 and the chosen playwrights will be contacted before Christmas, 2016. We produce Full-length plays and musicals, no one-acts or children's plays.

Y.E.S. (Year-End Series) Play Festival, Cont.

We are now approaching our 18th festival scheduled for April, 2017. The brochures containing the Guidelines and an Entry Form (which MUST accompany all submissions) are in the process of being designed and will be mailed in February, 2016.

Requests for the official brochure should be sent to forman@nku.edu or addressed to:
Professor Sandra Forman
c/o N.K.U. Theatre & Dance,
Fine Arts 205
Highland Heights, KY 41099

We do not accept electronic submissions. Playwrights should submit scripts and the required entry form to:
Corrie Danieley
NKU Theatre & Dance
Fine Arts 229
Highland Heights, KY 41099

Kentucky Venues for Self-Producing Playwrights

Editor's Note: Playwrights wishing to self-produce their own plays may wish to enquire about doing so at one or more of the following venues. Most assuredly these are not the only such venues; they are the ones familiar to the editor.

Cynthiana

The Roh's Opera House 133 E. Pike Street, Cynthiana, KY 41031, is home to the 400-seat auditorium and balcony theater and to Aeolian Hall, a rehearsal space. For information and to rent either facility call (859) 234-9803

Lexington

Downtown Arts Center (DAC) 141 E. Main St, Lexington, KY 40507 is home to a 250-seat Black Box Theatre, rehearsal space and meeting rooms, office space and the DAC Box Office. For information and to rent the facility please contact Celeste Lewis at clewis2@lexingtonky.gov or call (859)425-2349.

The Lyric Theatre & Cultural Arts Center 300 E. Third Street, Lexington, KY 40507 has a 530-seat auditorium ideal for movies, concerts and performances. For information about the facility and how to rent it visit http://www.lexingtonlyric.com/rental.html for rate sheets, specifications and other information or call (859)280-2201.

Louisville

The Bard's Town, 1801 Bardstown Road, Louisville, KY: A 62-seat upstairs theatre well suited to small shows. This facility is booked a year or more in advance so plan ahead. Contact via information on its website at http://www.thebardstowntheatre.org/ or by calling Doug Schutte at the theatre at (502)749-5275.

Henry Clay Theatre, 604 S. Third Street, 3rd Floor, Louisville, KY. The space is home to the Bunbury Theatre Company and Pandora Productions. For rates and information email Kent Weyland at KWeyland@citypropertiesgroup.com.

Kentucky Center for the Performing Arts, 501 W. Main Street, Louisville, KY hosts three theatres, any of which are available for rent, including Whitney Hall, with 2,406 seats; Bomhard Theatre, with 619 seats; and the Boyd Martin Theatre (also known as the MeX), with 139 seats. Additionally, the Kentucky Center for the Arts administers a separate facility, Brown Theatre, with 1,400 seats located eight blocks away. For more information call (502)562-0100 or visit the website kentuckycenter.org.

The Vault 1031: Performing Arts Venue, 1031 S. 6th St (Zane), Louisville. For more information or to book either/both the Rehearsal Hall or Armored Car Theatre contact either Jon Huffman, Director, Co. Artistic Director via huffcull@msn.com (email) or phone (502)386-8992 (cell) OR Barbara Cullen, Co-Artistic Director, Program Coordinator via barbara.cullen117@gmail.com (email) or phone (502)500-1131 (cell).

Paducah

Market House Theatre, 132 Market House Square has four spaces available for event rental. Check their detailed online event pricing guide at http://markethousetheatre.org/facility-rental. Contact Facilities Manager Travis Hensel, thensel@mhtplay.com, (270)444-6828 ext. 213 for more information.

Contributors:

Steve Cleberg has been the Director of Theatre Arts at Somerset Community College since 1986. Two of his plays, ***Radio Suspense Theatre: The First Episode*** and ***Radio Suspense Theatre***, are published by Playscripts Inc. His first musical, ***Tin Pan Alley Tavern***, was produced in the fall of 2014.

A. K. (Angela) Forbes holds an MA in professional writing and editing from the University of Cincinnati. She serves on the board of Village Players in Fort Thomas, Kentucky and is a member of Cincinnati Playwrights Initiative. Angela's plays have been produced locally by several groups and selected nationally by SourceFest (Washington, D.C.), Association for Theatre in Higher Education (ATHE) and the Rockford, Illinois New Play Festival. She is a three-time finalist for the Heideman Award (Actors Theatre of Louisville).

Nancy Gall-Clayton, Metro Louisville, has had plays read or produced at nearly 100 venues. She was a Tennessee Williams Scholar at Sewanee Writers Conference and is published by Dramatic Publishing, Smith & Kraus, Meriwether, Motes, and others. She teaches at Shape & Flow Writing Instruction (safws.com). Nancy belongs to the International Centre for Women Playwrights, Kentucky Playwrights Workshop, Cherokee Roundtable, and Southeastern Theatre Conference. She serves as the Dramatists Guild's Kentucky representative.

Michael W. Hatton is a freelance director and stage manager who serves as the Theatre and Dance Program Head for NKU's School of the Arts. Favorite credits include director of ***Moby Dick: Rehearsed, The Wedding Singer, Grease!, The Farnsworth Invention, The Rocky Horror Show, The American Clock, The Oresteia; The Santaland Diaries*** (New Edgecliff Theatre); ***Eastbound Jungle*** (Cincinnati Fringe Festival). Mr. Hatton has also worked with several regional companies including Showstoppers/Belterra Casino, Cincinnati Men's Chorus, and the New Edgecliff Theatre.

Philip Paradis is Playwright-in-Residence at Manhattan Repertory Theatre. His plays have been produced in NY, CA, KY, OH, RI, and WA. His awards include the Cincinnati Directors Competition Grand Prize for ***Footprints of the Polar Bear***, and The Audience Choice Award at 24 EXPERIMENT, Point Loma Actors Theater, San Diego, CA. He has served on the faculties of Northern Kentucky University, Iowa State University, Western Carolina University, and Oklahoma State University.

Appendix: Historical Data

Kentucky New Play Series: Plays produced at the Kentucky State Fair
Kentucky Playwrights Workshop, Inc., producing organization, 2014-2015
Bill McCann, Jr., independent producer, 2012-2013

2015
Rose Upon a White Gait by Tammy Brady
Wash Day by Sarah Diamond Burroway
Flight Path by A.K. Forbes
Zombie Love by Jennifer Johnson
Namaste by Stephanie Porter

2014
Reindeer by Richard Cavendish
A Curiosity Quilt by Nancy Gall-Clayton
My Father Thinks He's Irish by George McGee
Sunny Side by Philip Paradis
When Grandma Davis Hit the **Glass** by Rebecca Ryland
Visitation Privileges by Brian Walker

2013
The Engagement by George McGee
A Life in the Day of Robert/Robby by Tim Soulis
The Past is Not Past by Gary Eldridge

2012
Outings by Mary Christopher Grogan
Three O'clock by Bill McCann, Jr.

Roots of the Bluegrass New Play Contest and Festival
Kentucky Theatre Association

2015
Full-length Play Finalists:
Boxes by Catherine Goguen & J. Michael Radford
Poor Little Edward by Cody Taylor
CPR on the Lost Continent by Brian Walker (Winner)

10 Minute Play Winner
Roscoe-N-Junebug by Steven R. Bond

2014
Full-length Play Finalists:
A Passing Moment by John Kelly
According to John by David John Preece
The Prince of Riker's Island by Mike Meadors (Winner)

Inaugural 10-Minute Play Winner:
Strangers in the Park by Morgan Patton

2013
Finalists:
A Closet in Kentucky by Justin Ayer
A Certain Grace by Teresa Jenkins (Teresa Lee Fowler)
Dog by Brian Walker (Winner)

2012
Finalists:
Sex Again by Heidi Saunders
FB: A Ghost Story by Brian Walker
The Room by Jim Inman (Winner)

2011
Finalists:
Sumbahdee by Donna Phillips
Crossing the Line by Toni Wiley
The Pictures by Gary Eldridge (Winner)

2010
Finalists:
Pump Works by Heidi Saunders
A Fine Year for Mushrooms by Elizabeth Shear Orendorff
Papa and Blue Angel by Clarence Hettinger (Winner)

2009
Finalists:
Gone Astray by Walter May
Bernice Sizemore's 70th Birthday by Nancy Gall-Clayton
Aiden's Gift by Elizabeth Shear Orendorff (winner)

The Ten-Tucky Contest and Festival of New Plays
The Bard's Town Theatre
Doug Schutte, Producer

2015
A Dramatic Work, Signifying Nothing by Jon Becraft
It's Just a Box by Sarah Diamond Burroway
Film Noir by Andy Epstein
Levels of Living by Nancy Gall-Clayton
Hero Worship by Brian Walker
The Interview by Rebecca Ryland
Whistler's Mother by Doug Schutte
Reunion by Gary Wadley

2014
Action and Interaction by Corey Music
All the Answers by Mark Cornell
BSFFs by Bryce Woodard
Edgar by David Clark
Rose by Valerie Powell
Shop at Home by Tara Anderson
The Bubble by Taj Whitesell
The Library by Gary Wadley

2013
A Trip to Eden by Nancy Gall-Clayton
Out of the Closet by J.R. Greenwell
Properly Served by Bill Forsyth
The Rental Company by Mark Cornell
Hunting Jackalopes by Ben Unwin
A Day on the Savannah by Gary Wadley
Threesome by Brian Walker
That One Time Eric Clapton Sold His Soul to the Devil by Patrick Wensink

2012
Judging Quilts by Trish Ayers
Gay Encounters of the Third Kind by Andrew Epstein
Aphrodite at the ER by Nancy Gall-Clayton
Nightstalker & Canary by Ben Gierhart
Sweet Virginia by Erin Keane
Stained Glass by Doug Schutte
Finn's Motel by Brian Walker
A Falling Piano with Your Name on It by Patrick Wensink

2011
Wedding for Godot by Andrew Epstein
Encounter at The Ink Spot by Nancy Gall-Clayton
The Intruder by Tom Kerrigan
Over by Alex Lee Morse
Love Religiously by Doug Schutte
Neighborly Do's and Don'ts by Brian Walker
The Internet President by Patrick Wensink
Disappearances, or The Groom's Shoes by Nadeem
    Zaman

The Next Issue

Kentucky Theatre Yearbook, 2017 will contain a listing of all plays by Kentucky Playwrights given readings/productions anywhere in the world, PLUS readings/productions within Kentucky by playwrights from outside Kentucky, plus articles:

1. Articles about:
   - Sallie Bingham
   - Marsha Norman
   - Suzan-Lori Parks
   - Naomi Wallace
   - George C. Wolfe
2. Craft articles about playwriting, or of interest to playwrights
3. An article about the Kentucky Theatre Trail
4. An article about the Kentucky Humanities Council's Kentucky Chautauqua program, focused on how one/more playwright-actors developed their script/s and character/s
5. Reviews of new plays by Kentucky playwrights (review to not exceed 100 words and focused on the SCRIPT, not the performances/direction—except as the direction or performances indicate the ability to perform/bring the script effectively to life)
6. Other subjects for articles considered with queries received by August 1, 2016
7. One or more short plays (10-30 pages, each)
8. New listings for the Contests and Opportunities section

Submission deadline is October 15, 2016 for articles, and January 1, 2017 for plays that have performance dates on and/or after that date. A play that opens on December 31 must be submitted by email not later than midnight January 1, 2017.

Queries only required of those wishing to be paid, all others can send complete article in exchange for complimentary copy upon publication. Submissions/queries to:

JW Books, PO Box 143, Cynthiana, KY 41031
Payment/copies sent upon publication.

Byline given for articles and reviews but not for Contests or Opportunities

Estimated 2017 publication date: The Ides of March, 2017

No payment or copies given for reviews or for listings for the "Contests and Opportunities" sections.

New for the 2017 Issue

Classified Advertising: Advertisements of goods and services of help to the community of Kentucky theatres and playwrights will be accepted on a first-come, first-served basis at a rate of $20 for 40 words and $0.50 per word for each additional word.

Kentucky Playwrights Corner: Members of Kentucky Playwrights Workshop, Inc. (KPW) may have a short bio or contact information of up to 40 words included in the next issue free of charge, and $0.50 for each additional word. This offer is limited to the first 50 full or associate members of KPW to submit their entry and payment, if any. DEADLINE: September 1, 2016.

Display Advertising: Full, half-page and quarter-page advertisements of goods and services of help to the community of Kentucky theatres and playwrights will be accepted on a first-come, first-served basis. Discounts are given to theatres or producers advertising readings or productions of plays by Kentucky playwrights and/or full/associate members of KPW.

HELP WANTED

Advisory Board Members: Must have an interest in helping discover writers and potential advertisers for Kentucky Theatre Yearbook and attending an annual meeting of the Advisory Board to give advice and insight to the editorial staff. This is a volunteer position with no more than two such members from each Kentucky congressional district; members to be listed in each issue. Members serve non-renewable two year terms. Meetings to rotate around the state. Members will receive a free copy of the Kentucky Theatre Yearbook during each year of service.

Writers, paid and unpaid:

Paid writers should be professional in behavior and quality of submissions. Such writers must submit clippings and well-reasoned written queries that indicate an ability to write an appropriate article and successfully complete that article on time. Pay to be negotiated at the time query is accepted, but not to exceed 25 cents per word. Pay will be upon publication. Kill fee equal to one quarter of agreed fee. Expenses may be negotiated at time query is accepted but will not exceed $100. Initially, writers whose prior writing experience is academic and not for newspapers or other popular media will not be paid.

Unpaid writers will include individuals without experience writing for newspapers or other popular media. Additionally, *individuals submitting reviews, Contests, Festivals, or Opportunities* will not be paid. However, individuals writing reviews whose review is subsequently published will receive a copy of the issue to a maximum of two free copies.

Reviewers will be expected to turn in reviews not to exceed 100 words discussing the quality of the script and how well it translates to the stage. Mentions of directing, performances, designers, etc. should only be in relation to the ability of the playwright's vision to be translated to the stage. Not all reviews will be published and only the authors of published reviews will receive a copy of the issue.

Advertising Sales Representatives: 100% commission. Sales period April 1- October 1, 2016. Protected territories may be offered to those representatives generating $5,000 in gross advertising revenue in a given area within 90 days. Good commission rates. A great summer job for theatre or arts administration students or teachers. Contact us for more information at ky.playwright@yahoo.com; Put "Ad Rep" in the subject line.

NOTICES

Amateur and professional performance rights to *Dividing Adam's Ashes* are held by its playwright, A.K. Forbes. To secure performance rights please contact Ms. Forbes at 17 S. Shaw Lane, Ft. Thomas, KY 41075, emailangelakf@yahoo.com. Only the playwright can set the terms for performances of her play, or negotiate or collect royalties therefor.

Amateur and professional performance rights to *Sunny Side* are held by its playwright, Philip Paradis. To secure performance rights please contact Mr. Paradis, 22 Sterling Avenue, Ft. Thomas, KY 41075, phil.paradis@fuse.net, (859)653-6344. Only the playwright can set the terms for performances of his play, or negotiate or collect royalties therefor.

Submissions

Playwrights may submit information (email ky.playwright @yahoo.com) for the next issue:
- Any playwright residing anywhere in the world who had a reading or production IN KENTUCKY of a new stage play during calendar year 2016 may submit information about such readings or productions (send name of play, name of playwright, name of venue produced at, name of Kentucky city)

- Any KENTUCKY playwright who has a reading or production of a new stage play ANYWHERE IN THE WORLD during calendar year 2016 may submit information about such readings or productions (send name of play, name of playwright, name of venue produced at, city and state or country)

Theatres or playwrights may submit contest, festival, or opportunity information for next issue to ky.playwright@yahoo.com:
- Name of contest
- Name of sponsoring organization
- Address, City, State, Zip Code
- Email address
- Website
- Phone number
- Contact person
- Rules/how to obtain rules
- How to submit script
- Deadline
- Maximum length, 200 words TOTAL
- Space considerations will determine how many contests, festivals, and opportunities will appear in next year's Yearbook
- All submissions subject to editing for length and clarity

About the Editor

Bill McCann, Jr. is an advocate for Kentucky playwrights. He is a playwright, producer and poet, editor, publisher and teacher. He has started and regularly attends writing groups in Cynthiana and Corinth. He was a founder and is the current president of Kentucky Playwrights Workshop, Inc. Mr. McCann founded the Kentucky New Play Series and has been its producer from 2012 to the present. From 2012 through 2014 he served on the board of the Kentucky Theatre Association as Contest Coordinator of the Roots of the Bluegrass New Play Contest.

Currently, Mr. McCann is Playwright Mentor for the Carnegie Center for Literacy & Learning, Lexington. He is a member of Actors & Playwrights Collaborative, as well as of the Dramatist Guild of America. McCann is adjunct faculty at Bluegrass Community & Technical College, Lexington and Winchester where he teaches developmental English. Mr. McCann holds an MEd from the University of Virginia and an MA in theatre from the University of Kentucky. He and Jeanine Grant Lister live at Roxford Farm near Corinth, in northwest Harrison County, Kentucky with (currently) four cats and Halligan the Wonder Dog.

Bulk Discounts

Discounts of up to 40% off
the regular price are available to individuals
and businesses that
purchase a minimum of
five (5) copies of the
Kentucky Theatre Yearbook, 2016

Individuals and businesses purchasing in
quantities of ten (10) or more will not be
charged for shipping and handling

For more information contact:
JW Books
PO Box 143
Cynthiana, KY 41031

or by email at
Ky.playwright@yahoo.com

www.ingramcontent.com/pod-product-compliance
Lightning Source LLC
Chambersburg PA
CBHW070811100426
42742CB00012B/2326